But I'm Not a Reading Teacher!

BUT I'M NOT A READING TEACHER!

Literacy Strategies for Career and Technical Educators

By Sandra Adams and
Gwendolyn Leininger

But I'm Not a Reading Teacher!

Copyright by Sandra Adams and Gwendolyn Leininger 2017

First published in 2017

The rights of Sandra Adams and Gwendolyn Leininger to be identified as the authors of this work have been asserted in accordance with the Copyright Designs and Patents Act of 1988.

All rights reserved.

This book is sold subject to the condition that it shall not, by way of trade or otherwise, be reproduced, stored in a retrieval system, be lent, resold, hired out, or otherwise circulated or transmitted without the authors' prior consent in any form of binding or cover other than that in which it is published and without a similar condition, including this condition, being imposed on the subsequent purchaser.

Cover design by Gwendolyn Leininger

Interior graphics by Abigaille Kizer and John Jehl

Interior photos taken by Gwendolyn Leininger, Sandra Adams, or Dean Meyer, or public domain.

SandyandGwen.com

Sandra Adams

Gwendolyn Leininger

But I'm Not a Reading Teacher! Literacy Strategies for Career and Technical Educators

ISBN-13:
978-1542869881

ISBN-10:
1542869889

First published in the United States of America
FIRST EDITION

CONTENTS

Acknowledgments	vii
Authors	viii

Introductory Materials

Introduction	1
The CTE Advantage	3
Before You Begin: Seven Principles	6
How to Use This Book	10

PART 1: INTEGRATED VOCABULARY — 13

Vocabulary for the CTE Classroom	15

Step 1 – Introduce — 19

Student-Led Word List (Lab Version)	20
Student-Led Word List (Reading Version)	22
Annotation System	24
Meaning Prediction Chart	26
Meaning Prediction through Think-Pair-Share	28
Notecard Chunking (Identifying Terms in Context)	30
Prediction Guide (Vocabulary Version)	32

Step 2 – Practice — 35

Forced Lab Conversation	36
Reflective Dictionary	38
Technology Games	42
Two-Column Notes	44
Nine Diamond Organizer	46

Step 3 – Explore Relationships — 49

Affinity Diagram (Categorizing Words)	50
Cause-Effect Chart	54
Refine and Define Chart (Writing Concise Definitions)	58
Flow Chart for Vocabulary Process Terms	60
Word Tree	64
Word Map (Identifying Attributes of Terms)	66
Connected Categories	68
CTE Vocabulary Grid	70

Step 4 – Deepen Understanding with SWRL — 73

Diagnosing Problems While Performance Testing in the Lab	74
Thirty-Second Talkabout	80
Entrance and Exit Cards	82
WebQuest Your Career Path	84
Incidental and Assessment Vocabulary	87

PART 2: PRODUCTIVE TALK — 89

What is Productive Talk? — 90
Physical Tools for Productive Talk — 95
Seven Norms for Discussion — 97

- *Carousel* — 98
- *Post-It Note Tug-of-War* — 100
- *Gather the Facts* — 102
- *Paired Reading* — 104
- *Question Fishbowl* — 106
- *Affinity Diagram (Brainstorming in Categories)* — 110
- *Flow Chart (Brainstorming Processes)* — 114
- *Concept Map (Brainstorming Attributes and Features)* — 120
- *Decision Tree (Brainstorming to Analyze)* — 124
- *Five Whys (Brainstorming the Roots of a Problem)* — 128
- *Cause-Effect Brainstorming* — 134
- *SWOT Analysis (Brainstorming through Different Lenses)* — 140
- *Choices and Consequences* — 142
- *Teacher Activity: Feedback Prediction Guide* — 144

PART 3: DISCIPLINARY LITERACY — 147

What Is Disciplinary Literacy? — 148
Developing Your Goals for Disciplinary Literacy Instruction — 150
Planning Strategies for Disciplinary Literacy Instruction — 151

Disciplinary Literacy: Big Ideas — 153

- *Writing Prompt Carousel* — 154
- *Specified Summary (Guided Note-Taking)* — 160
- *Bigwig Bio* — 164
- *Prediction Guide (Disciplinary Literacy Version)* — 168
- *Video Close Reading* — 172
- *Professional Interview* — 174

Disciplinary Literacy: Habits of Mind — 177

- *Real-World Scenarios* — 178
- *Career Curator* — 180
- *Know Your Target Market* — 182
- *Informational Speech* — 184
- *Punch the Holes in It* — 188
- *Reading Schematics, Diagrams, and Blueprints (Text Features)* — 190
- *Examining Ethics* — 194
- *Professional Work Ethic* — 196

APPENDIX A – Choosing Complex Text — 201
APPENDIX B – Multiple Intelligences Test — 202
APPENDIX C – Common Core Literacy Standards for Science and Technical Subjects — 206
INDEX — 211

Acknowledgments

This work is a collaborative effort by two authors who have drawn on the practical wisdom of countless others. Thank you to the educational visionaries, researchers, and authors whose work has helped us understand instruction and the role of teacher effectiveness in student achievement. We have been especially inspired by the work of John Hattie, Robert Marzano, Mike Rutherford, and Barak Rosenshine. Many authors and presenters have inspired us to think innovatively, especially Rachael Mann, Adam Grant, and Daniel Pink.

Innovation often means building on the work of others. Thank you to the educators whose work provided a foundational structure for this book and then helped us refine our ideas, and especially to those who allowed us to share their instructional approaches: Karen Gillie, Lisa Schaefer, Jon Capps, Veronica Townes, Darrell Wattley, and Kim Swain.

Thank you to Larry Gerardot for making our partnership possible. Thank you to Cindy McKinney with Region 8 Education Service Center for suggesting that we follow our own advice and cater to multiple learning styles, making our book format more accessible with links to a variety of digital media. And thank you to Dena Irwin with the Indiana Department of Education for believing in our work and supporting our purpose.

Lastly, we have been bolstered by the strength of those closest to us, without whose support we could not have carried out this work. We are grateful to our husbands and children for their support, enthusiasm, and love.

This book is dedicated to the innovative staff and administration at the Career Academy at Anthis in Fort Wayne, Indiana. Thank you for your inspiring commitment to excellence in educating young people.

Authors

Sandra Adams is a veteran teacher, entrepreneur, and instructional coach at the Career Academy at Anthis in Fort Wayne, Indiana. She was a Race to the Top team member, and she leads professional development workshops for local teachers. Sandra lives with her husband and three daughters.

Gwendolyn Leininger is a freelance writer, independent editor, and public school advocate in Fort Wayne, Indiana. She works with Sandra Adams to compile research and write materials for local educators. Gwendolyn lives with her husband and one daughter.

But I'm Not a Reading Teacher!

Introduction

This book isn't about getting your automotive students to journal or turning your agriculture students into bookworms. It is about helping your students improve their literacy in ways that are distinctly relevant to your career field.

Literacy is king these days. All educators, regardless of what subjects they teach, are expected to help students improve their literacy learning. Maybe you're on board, maybe not. Perhaps you'd really like to spend time on your area of expertise and leave literacy to the ELA teachers. That's understandable, but if you want your students to be successful in your subject area, reading and its associated skills are your tools, not a separate subject to learn. There's no getting around it: reading, writing, speaking, listening, and thinking skills—all of which are included in the modern understanding of literacy—are vital for success in school and in life. Literacy is so tied to outcomes that we even see its connection to incarceration rates: students who don't read at grade level by the end of third grade are four times less likely to graduate (six times less likely if they are low-income)—and if they don't graduate high school, they are 63 times more likely to go to prison than college graduates! (Hernandez, 2012; Sum et. al., 2009). You can help students to improve their general literacy and become literate in your content area—what we refer to as *disciplinary literacy*—by incorporating and adapting the activities in this book. We will suggest beginning with your approach to vocabulary instruction (part 1), incorporating active *productive talk* strategies (part 2), and paying specific attention to what literacy means in your discipline (part 3).

Literacy skills are your tools, not a separate subject to learn.

The What and The How

It has always been true that advanced literacy skills help students learn more, in any subject. The problem is that you don't have time to teach reading and writing when you have your own set of content area standards to reach. Here's the good news: you can do both with a What/How approach.

Maybe graphic design, not literacy, is *what* you teach, but literacy can be the *how*. Using broad literacy skills, graphic organizers, and adaptable literacy-based lessons as the "how" is called *content area literacy*. This book includes many ideas for content area literacy, but it also continues further, into *disciplinary literacy*. Disciplinary literacy is the idea that literacy means something specific within each content area (Shanahan & Shanahan, 2011). This book will help you think through what it means to be literate in your discipline, so that you can purposefully identify the literacy skills you hope to teach. How does a successful adult in your career field use speaking, writing, reading, listening, and

Your content area is *what* you teach, but literacy can be the *how*.

thinking skills? You probably already include many of these skills in the way you teach graphic design or welding or nursing: students read a textbook, and they follow written step-by-step instructions, for example. Those are literacy skills, and there are many more literacy skills your students can exercise to enhance their graphic design learning.

One goal of this book is to help you define literacy for your classroom and identify the literacy skills you are already teaching. For instance, cosmetology, EMT, and IT professionals think sequentially, and you would see this in their approach to literacy, whereas early childhood and multimedia classes emphasize divergent thinking skills. The graphics on the following pages can get you started. We also refer to specific Common Core State Standards throughout the book, so that you will be prepared to explain to your students and administrators exactly how you are incorporating disciplinary literacy into your classroom.

For more on disciplinary literacy, see part 3 of this book. You can also scan the QR code to the left to access printable posters that may help you define disciplinary literacy for your classroom.

> **Common Core Connection**
>
> You'll see boxes like this with each activity, to help you determine which literacy standards might be achieved with that activity. But keep in mind that these activities are adaptable and could be used toward many standards in different ways.

Keeping it Hands-On

As a Career and Technical Education (CTE) teacher, you're in a uniquely privileged position with students who are interested in a career in your content area. You can help them improve their overall literacy simply by fine-tuning the *how* of your content-area instruction to develop disciplinary literacy. There are many creative ways to use literacy skills as the "how" in your teaching. This book explores one that we think is often overlooked: productive talk. By *productive talk*, we mean conversations in which students do most of the talking, while teachers guide them to listen to each other, explain their thinking, question and challenge each other's ideas, and revise their own opinions based on input from others.

We in CTE are often hesitant to engage in literacy learning because we don't want to lose the hands-on learning time that is essential to career preparation. So many students thrive with an emphasis on hands-on learning, and the last thing we want to do is make CTE classrooms more like traditional ones. Instead, we want to encourage a student-led, engaging approach to literacy learning that considers multiple learning styles. Productive talk can be an effective tool for literacy learning while maintaining an active, engaged, hands-on learning environment. Every strategy in this book allows for blended learning styles and the communication skills that are needed for 21st century careers. Part two of this book specifically explains more about productive talk and provides a collection of classroom strategies that are especially conducive to it.

The CTE Advantage

CTE programs are known for offering hands-on learning that keeps students engaged. In fact, the national average graduation rate for students in CTE programs is 93 percent, compared to the average freshman graduation rate of 80 percent (ACTE, 2017). The key to CTE success is the lab.

Students choose CTE because it is practical and relevant. Career field lab experience is just that—it is EXPERIENCE. In the lab, students routinely problem-solve, analyze parts and processes, move around, manipulate objects, operate tools, and actively collaborate to build knowledge from different sources. Hands-on work in a lab allows students to reach a "flow" as they work on something that is meaningful and practical to them. They're in their element.

Lab + Classroom = The CTE Advantage

As CTE students walk to the lab portion of a class, they are lively. There is an apparent eagerness, a momentum in their step. But upon hearing "Let's go back to the classroom," that same group of students loses momentum, preparing for what many of them have come to regard as boring. The problem for many of them is a psychological occurrence called *habituation*. Habituation occurs when the brain has experienced something so often that it no longer fires dopamine, the chemical that signals pleasure or reward. When we've stopped feeling emotional rewards from classroom experiences, we lose engagement. Think of the word "worksheet" or "study guide." By a student's junior year, these words hardly fire up excitement.

To combat habituation, take advantage of what CTE programs do best and bring the lab into your classroom. Here's how:

- **Chunking**: Segment each lesson to create opportunities for dynamic combinations of classroom and lab work. Chunking ensures you don't lecture beyond students' attention spans.
- **Blended learning**: Use that chunking to "swirl" between speaking, writing, reading, and listening activities, including digital media and—you guessed it—plenty of hands-on learning.

The activities in this book will help make your classroom more dynamic, but be sure to combine them with elements of your own lab work that you have found to be successful. On the next two pages, you'll see specific tips for avoiding habituation in your classroom, as well as one example of a lesson designed this way.

Avoiding Habituation

1. **Watch your words.** If you hear yourself saying words like study guide, worksheet, quiz, and textbook all the time, consider coming up with an alternative activity, form of text, or assessment style.
2. **Bring physical tools and parts into the classroom.** As often as possible, allow students to handle parts, pass around tools or stand around you as you lecture—creating more of a discussion or demonstration.
3. **Chunk your instruction.** Breaking class time into segments increases the overall attentiveness of your students and makes it easier to add variety.
4. **Pay attention to equity.** Every student should have the opportunity to participate in discussion, prediction, or answering a question. We are always more attentive when we've made a prediction or offered our best answer. See page 95 for a list of physical tools that give every student an opportunity to answer.
5. **Use graphic organizers well.** Instead of treating charts and visuals as "extras," build lessons around them, using them to encourage students to collaborate and explain their thinking process during the lesson. Graphic organizers promote high quality conversation during and after activities.
6. **Use writing differently.** There are hundreds of ways to write other than an essay. Make writing a tool for constructing meaning; providing descriptive and directive feedback; preparing visuals, videos, and graphic organizers; and creating useful content within your career field.
7. **Rearrange people.** Continually change how information is shared and discussed. Within each hour of learning, try to have 2-3 different arrangements:
    a. whole group
    b. small group
    c. triads
    d. partners
    e. individual work while teacher meets with students one-on-one
    f. teacher-led discussion
    g. think-pair-share

Sample In-Classroom Chunked Lesson Plan
HVAC Classroom

Here's an overview of what a chunked and blended lesson that includes the literacy strategies in this book might look like. Any teacher can use this overview as a guide to structuring lessons. You can also view several sample lesson plans for specific classes on our website by scanning this QR code.

Time	Activity
15 min	**Bell Ringer Challenge** (Individual work; whole-class discussion) Students examine the manufacturer claims on efficiency and customer satisfaction from different manufacturer guides. Students use Concept Maps (see p.120) to write 4 features of the efficiency claims for each manufacturer guide. Finish with short whole-class discussion on selection of features, comparing student thinking.
20-30 min	**SWOT analysis** (see p.140) (paired work; whole-class discussion) Teacher describes a process that students will investigate with text & Internet. Students are paired, read designated pages of text, and work to solve the challenges. Teacher facilitates and supports as students complete the SWOT. Pairs share out as a whole class.
10 min	**30-second talkabout** (see p.80) (paired work) Students engage in feedback over the reading using 30-second talkabout. Prompt 1: Talker, tell your partner the strengths and opportunities of the high efficiency design, based on what you just learned. Prompt 2: Next talker, tell your partner how the weaknesses you found could be improved upon.
15-20 min.	**Listening/Observing** (teacher-led discussion – lecture with some questioning) Teacher leads notes on Module 4, power point and textbook, with a high-efficiency design part on display or passed around. Students encouraged to take sketch notes (p.162) or two-column notes (p. 44).
25 min	**Quizlet Live** (small group work) In small groups of 3-4, assigned randomly by Quizlet.com (see p. 42), students play Quizlet.Live game sessions over the new vocabulary terms and previously learned terms to make connections.
10 min	**Transition to Lab** (whole-class discussion) Teacher leads discussion of any missed terms from the game and clears up misunderstandings before moving to the lab session of class Students are given lab task and discuss how the lab work relates to the content and vocabulary focus from today

Before You Begin: Seven Principles

1. Broaden your understanding of the word "text."

Don't use only the textbook for your students' reading. Make learning more engaging and effective for CTE students by using other texts that are relevant to the students' lives and the content area. The Common Core Literacy Standards are content-neutral, so you can work on the literacy standards and your own content standards at the same time. Find articles from trade magazines and journals. Use advertising material as text, and have students analyze its claims. Have students read a complicated technical manual and translate it, writing or speaking as though they were explaining to a layperson. As you choose texts, keep in mind the foundations of literacy instruction (phonics, phonemic awareness, fluency, vocabulary, and comprehension [National Reading Panel 2000 qtd. In Johnson, 2008]), and try to choose texts that will be just challenging enough to keep students engaged while still allowing them to construct meaning. Use a business's website as "text," and examine the intent and claims of its author. You can even treat a video or an in-class demonstration as a text and an opportunity to practice literacy skills. See page 201 for more detailed resources on choosing complex text for your classroom.

2. Broaden your understanding of the word "literacy."

Dictionaries may define *literacy* as simply reading and writing, but for the educator its definition is much broader. Because a modern understanding of literacy includes skills such as presenting and finding evidence in a text, you have a lot of flexibility as you make literacy the *how* of your instruction. It includes more than reading. Encourage critical literacy as it relates to your content area. Look at the speaking, writing, listening, and presenting that your students already do, and hone those activities to boost literacy learning. See part 3 and page 150 (Redefine Literacy for CTE) for a more in-depth look at modern literacy skills.

3. Create a classroom library.

This can be especially helpful in a CTE classroom because your students will encounter libraries more often in traditional classrooms, and often they will be filled with works of fiction. Yet in any career field there are helpful books, articles, magazines, and historical resources. Introduce students to the publications they will see in their chosen career field. Collect materials that show the history of the career field (for example, in an IT class, historical manuals, advertisements, and even parts for older-model computers may prove more interesting and inspiring than the textbook itself). Print and collect individual newspaper articles about advances in your field and innovative companies.

4. Teach Reading Skills Without Reading

Of course, your students should read, but they don't always have to have their noses in a book to learn important reading skills. Important literacy skills—like making predictions, brainstorming, critically examining a source, etc.—can be part of hands-on learning too. ELA teachers use what they call "pre-reading" and "post-reading" strategies before and after reading to get students thinking about the text. You can adapt those same strategies for before and after any in-class activity to practice thinking skills. For example, an ELA teacher might use a graphic organizer or a brainstorming activity to help students make predictions before reading. Likewise, a CTE teacher could use the same graphic organizer or brainstorming activity before a laboratory demonstration. Afterwards, chart the information, craft summaries, hold panel discussions, debates, and interviews (all "post-reading" strategies). Encourage analysis and questioning during the class activity, just as an ELA teacher would during reading. These are all useful life skills that apply to any content area and carry over into literacy. Here are a few literacy skills you can practice even when your students are not reading:

- Brainstorm
- Identify background and purpose of source/author/demonstrator
- Identify cultural context
- Identify structure of text/demonstration
- Make predictions
- Make lists
- Write instructions
- Introduce unfamiliar vocabulary
- Ask questions
- Annotate
- Paraphrase
- Identify vocabulary in context
- Identify relationships between information
- Summarize
- Analyze cause-effect
- Discuss possible problems
- Discuss possible solutions

5. Communicate with your English Language Arts (ELA) teachers.

The content literacy standards are intended to supplement, not replace, the ELA literacy standards. Talk to your ELA teachers to find out which skills students struggle most to meet, and look for ways to incorporate them into your content area. Ask them about their favorite "pre-reading" and "post-reading" strategies, and adapt them to your own activities, as discussed above. Often CTE classes are so different from traditional ELA classes that your class may be well suited to working on skills that may be harder for ELA teachers to make time for.

6. *Tailor instruction to multiple learning styles*

Most teachers affirm the importance of engaging multiple learning styles, and CTE teachers especially are aware of the need for a less traditional academic approach. But with all the divergent factors teachers must consider when planning their lessons, considering multiple learning styles sometimes falls by the wayside. It is not uncommon for even great educators to inadvertently favor one or two types of intelligence over others in their teaching practice. We recommend taking a few minutes to quiz yourself and discover your own learning preferences, which may be your most natural teaching style. Scan at left for a short online quiz from Edutopia, or use the assessment included in Appendix B on page 202.

To help you avoid this pitfall, we have included instructional strategies that cater to a variety of learning styles. Because productive talk depends on the equitable inclusion of all students, it is especially important to take their individual ways of understanding into account. That doesn't mean you don't coax students out of their comfort zones or challenge them in their areas of weakness. It means instead that all students learn to adapt to a dynamic learning environment and you broaden their opportunities to contribute to the class.

Each activity in this book caters to multiple learning styles. Look for the icons from this chart in the sidebars to see which learning styles the activities engage most easily.

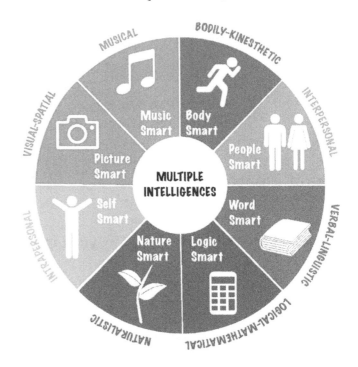

7. *SWRL every day*

If you "swirl" your lessons every day—that is, include an element of S̲peaking, W̲riting, R̲eading, and L̲istening—you'll be supporting literacy learning while working on your content area at the same time. This "swirl" doesn't have to take long and can be embedded into your hands-on lesson (WIDA Consortium, 2012).

One way to make time for SWRL daily is by chunking your instruction. Chunking means breaking down the lesson into manageable parts. We recommend chunking your instructional time as well as chunking longer texts to create built-in time for writing and discussion. More than a time-management strategy, chunking will help your students digest information and learn to engage actively with text.

The activities in this book are great ways to start SWRLing, but don't get caught up in the need for a special activity, and don't let cutesy names like "elbow partners" and "think-pair-share" scare you away. Just find ways you can incorporate daily speaking, writing, reading, and listening so that it fits your teaching style and comfort zone.

How to Use This Book

This book is organized into three parts, as follows:

Part 1: Integrated Vocabulary
This section explores the power of a systematized vocabulary instruction to structure your approach to content-area literacy. We suggest steps for teaching vocabulary, and within each step we provide several lesson ideas.

Part 2: Productive Talk
This section explains the power of active, student-led speaking activities for improving literacy. We provide lesson ideas that are especially conducive to productive talk.

Part 3: Disciplinary Literacy
This section looks more deeply at what literacy means within various CTE content areas and provides lesson ideas that can help you emphasize your students' growth as literate professionals within your field.

Connect to Standards and Goals

We include notes about how specific activities can help you emphasize the learning process over grades, encourage metacognition (thinking about thinking), and tailor instruction to multiple learning styles. These conditions are necessary for increasing engagement and getting the most out of productive talk. We further explain these goals in Part 2 on productive talk.

We include a "student perspective" quote at the end of many activities because it is important for students to find the work meaningful. In preparing any lesson, try to see it from the student's perspective so you can eliminate "busy work" and better explain the activity's purpose to students.

We also list the relevant Common Core literacy standards along with each activity. This should help you to connect what you are doing with the literacy skills being taught, to ensure that your students are getting the most out of their instructional time. The way you choose to adapt each activity will determine which standards you meet, and how thoroughly you meet them, but you can use the standards listed to get an idea of how you might use an activity. Page 206 features a complete list of Common Core literacy standards that are required for technical subjects. We hope our notes will help you to easily explain the "why" of the lesson to administrators, parents, and students.

Adapt It

These strategies are intended to be dynamic, changing in intensity and depth depending on your needs. You'll want to move between moments of teacher-directed and student-driven activity, allowing your students to engage at various times in expression, consultation, participation, partnership, activism, and leadership (Bray & McClaskey, 2016). These activities provide a platform for this kind of dynamic instruction, as long as you are willing to make them your own. As you adapt these and other strategies you come across, ask yourself the following guiding questions:

> How and when will students work together?
> How will I help students reflect on the significance of the information (text)?
> How can productive talk be used to deepen understanding?
> How and where can students engage in a genuine feedback exchange?
> How will the information be communicated to others?

This approach will require an open mind and some planning ahead, but it pays off in better student engagement and less trouble with discipline, and if you keep your plans organized you can use them year after year, minimizing the extra planning time. Think of the strategies in this book as suggestions and guidelines to help you find an approach to disciplinary literacy that works for you.

"As quick as…" You'll notice a note in the sidebar of each activity that gives you an idea of the minimum time required. But if you adapt these activities and include conversation, they may become much longer. The length of all these activities should vary according to your students' needs.

Approach It Holistically

While the individual strategies in this book can stand alone, they will be much more effective when you use them as part of a comprehensive approach to disciplinary literacy. Create long-term goals for your students' disciplinary literacy, and think of the individual lessons in this book as part of that larger plan.

Every strategy in this book can be useful to any CTE teacher, so we have not organized it by content area (strategies for agriculture teachers, strategies for cosmetology teachers, etc.). Instead, we hope you will choose a variety of activities that you can put into the context of your own discipline, keeping in mind your overall goal of disciplinary literacy.

Embrace Complexity

The kind of literacy learning that contemporary students need is critical literacy—an engagement with text that encourages thinking and questioning. Critical literacy gives power to the reader of a text to question the author's perspective and motives (McLaughlin & DeVoogd, 2004). Likewise, as you teach these literacy skills, you will be giving more power to your students, encouraging them to direct their own thinking and explore the nuances of whatever material they examine. Using critical literacy necessarily means no two lessons will be the same. The students will often be driving the lessons, and their interactions will move the class in different directions.

The concept of power is especially important in CTE classrooms because you will find so many examples in career fields of claims that are biased (advertisements, product claims, marketing materials, etc.). Part of teaching literacy is encouraging an understanding of the cultural themes represented in a text: for example, in a culinary class, student groups might examine various restaurants' websites and identify the target market and specific examples of language used to target that consumer group, then discuss the historical trends of particular styles of food and ingredients in various social classes. The possibilities are limitless for incorporating literacy learning into your CTE classroom. Embrace complexity and questioning, and then push students to be able to explain that complexity in their own words.

Complex Thought + Simple Communication

Richard Feynman, a Nobel Prize-winning physicist who worked on the atomic bomb and cracked safes, famously drove a 1975 Dodge van with squiggly lines painted on its sides. Those squiggles looked simple, but physicists know them as Feynman diagrams, which represent the very complex concept of quantum electrodynamics (QED). Feynman's deep understanding had allowed him to distill his knowledge down to the essentials to communicate it visually.

Those who understand complex ideas can explain them simply, in their own words. We recommend using graphic organizers and discussion time in the classroom to explore complex ideas, and then challenging students to paraphrase, perform, or represent those ideas in simple or unexpected ways. Summaries, graphic representations, and demonstrations are important, not in themselves, but because these simple ways of communicating require complex thought. As they seek to fit big ideas into their own words and new contexts, they take ownership of the material. As author Michael Shermer (2005) put it, "A visual display of data should be simple enough to fit on the side of a van."

PART 1: INTEGRATED VOCABULARY

IN THIS SECTION

Vocabulary Step 1: Introduce

    Student-Led Word List (Lab Version)
    Student-Led Word List (Reading Version)
    Annotation System
    Meaning Prediction Chart
    Meaning Prediction through Think-Pair-Share
    Notecard Chunking (Identifying Terms in Context)
    Prediction Guide (Vocabulary Version)

Vocabulary Step 2: Practice

    Forced Lab Conversations
    Reflective Dictionary
    Technology Games
    Two-Column Notes
    Nine Diamond Organizer

Vocabulary Step 3: Explore Relationships

    Affinity Diagram
    Cause-Effect Chart (Determining Word Relationships)
    Refine and Define Chart (Writing Concise Definitions)
    Flow Chart for Vocabulary Process Terms
    Word Tree
    Word Map (Identifying Attributes of Terms)
    Connected Categories
    CTE Vocabulary Grid

Vocabulary Step 4: Deepen Understanding with SWRL

    Diagnosing Problems While Performance Testing in the Lab
    Thirty-Second Talkabout
    Entrance and Exit Cards
    WebQuest Your Career Path
    Incidental and Assessment Vocabulary

But I'm Not a Reading Teacher!

Vocabulary for the CTE Classroom

"I need a vocabulary learning method that actually sticks!"

Begin with Vocabulary

If you'd like to move toward a more engaged and student-led classroom but you're not sure where to start, begin with vocabulary. Improving your approach to vocabulary can have a big impact, affecting content learning in all your lessons. Consider the book *Visible Learning*, John Hattie's groundbreaking synthesis of thousands of research studies on education. Hattie ranks 138 factors by how greatly they affect achievement—diverse factors such as teacher clarity, socioeconomic status, and early intervention, to name just a few—to show what the sum of the research says about their importance. Of all 138, vocabulary programs ranked 15th most effective, right after a student's prior achievement, and ahead of such buzzed-about topics as teacher professional development, home environment, socioeconomic status, and class size (Hattie, 2009, p. 297). More relevant to our focus on literacy is the finding that vocabulary programs had a greater effect than any other factor in the domain of curriculum, and their effect on reading comprehension was higher than any other literacy-focused topic.

Develop a Vocabulary Program

It has been widely acknowledged that effective vocabulary learning takes place in the context of reading and other classroom activities, rather than being taught in isolation. But that does not mean teachers should stop actively emphasizing vocabulary, using word lists, or designing vocabulary-specific lessons. You can't expect kids to adequately "pick up" vocabulary knowledge through their reading. The key is to approach those word lists with a sense of how important they really are, and to plan your use of them in correspondence with your broader focus on student-led productive talk and engaging teaching strategies. As a CTE teacher especially, your lessons likely include technical words that require intentional instruction for understanding. This reality, combined with Hattie's finding detailed above on the effectiveness of specific vocabulary strategies, underscores the need for developing and following a structured plan for teaching vocabulary. In fact, in several of the studies analyzed, the key element of the vocabulary programs' effectiveness was determined to be its structured and sequential nature.

The way you structure your vocabulary program can have a great effect on the way the rest of your lessons go. Your approach to teaching vocabulary can set the tone for how you want learning to happen in your class. Remember, many of the students in your CTE class are there because they want a non-traditional approach to learning. You want student engagement, so create a vocabulary program that is student-driven. According to Hattie's meta-analysis, the most effective vocabulary programs

- "provide both definitional and contextual information,
- involve students in deeper processing, and
- give students more than one or two exposures to the words they are to learn" (Hattie, 2009, p. 131-132).

In other words, you need to create a student-led, structured program that teaches vocabulary definitions **contextually**, **thoughtfully**, and **repeatedly**. We suggest that you follow the approach detailed below as you create vocabulary learning opportunities.

Cycle Your Vocabulary Program

We suggest a cyclical vocabulary program that includes four steps.

1. Introduce new words by allowing students to identify them during lessons that include previously-learned vocabulary.
2. Give students hands-on practice with defining and using the new words both in the classroom and in the lab.
3. Provide opportunities for students to explore the relationships between vocabulary words.
4. Deepen understanding by continually including vocabulary in all your content area's Speaking, Writing, Reading, and Listening activities (SWRL). Then add more new words into these activities to begin the cycle again.

Embrace Productive Talk

Each step of a successful vocabulary program should include SWRL activities. It is particularly important for students to engage in productive talk, speaking aloud for vocabulary learning. Research shows that a strong connection between the brain's speech centers is essential for learning new words (López-Barroso et. al., 2013). The vocabulary activities in this book, like all activities we share, are conducive to productive talk. You'll learn more about productive talk in Part 2 of this book.

The remainder of this Part 1 is devoted to breaking down these four steps and providing practical activities you can use within each.

But I'm Not a Reading Teacher!

VOCABULARY STEP 1: INTRODUCE

There are many ways to introduce vocabulary during a lesson that allows for engaging student involvement. This section includes several ideas, which you can adapt to your needs. Whatever method you choose, make sure it accomplishes these two goals:

1. Blurs the line between classroom and lab
2. Allows students to speak, write, read, and listen

Consider using lab activities as a platform for introducing vocabulary words, instead of handing out a word list during a separate classroom lesson. Have students write on clipboards during a demonstration, taking short breaks during the lab work to come up with definitions of vocabulary words or relationships between them. Or have them annotate a diagram periodically throughout the lab work. Then, back in the classroom, students will be more prepared to speak, write, read, and listen to each other's notes from the lab.

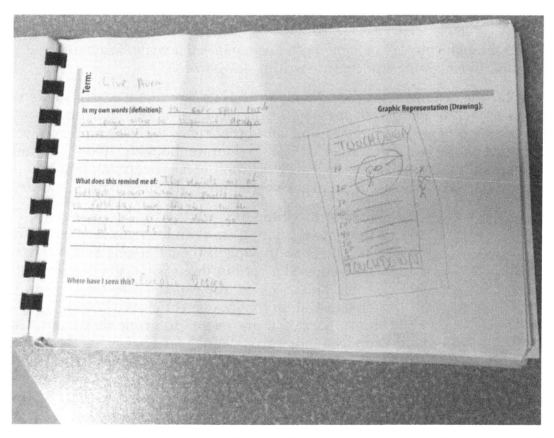

A student-made vocabulary booklet includes graphic representations of each term (see Reflective Dictionary on page 38).

Student-Led Word List (lab version)

Gist: Students create their own vocabulary list during lab work, connect the words to their prior knowledge, and use them in speaking and writing.

When to use: During a lab demonstration or video.

How It Works

Step 1: Preview your video or plan your lab demonstration to make sure it will include several unfamiliar words or concepts. If you wish, provide your students with a chart like that on p. 21 to help them organize their lists.

Step 2: Say, "Please bring your clipboards into the lab today. During our demonstration, listen for words that are unfamiliar and write them on your clipboards during the demonstration. Even if you understood the whole demonstration, try to write down at least 5 terms that are hard to explain. This isn't a test, and it's not for a grade—we just need to decide together which words to learn."

Step 3: Go through your lab demonstration or hands-on activity. Watching and pacing appropriately to make sure students are writing down words.

Step 4: After the demonstration say, "Now, write your best guess or explanation of the terms you've picked, using your memory of the demonstration. Sometimes writing it down helps us to figure out the meaning, and other times it shows us that a word we thought was familiar is a little harder to explain than we thought." Allow a few minutes for this step. TIP: Be sure to have students write their names on this and turn them in at the end of class, so you can use them to get a better understanding of prior knowledge.

The Why

As quick as: 20 minutes

Multiple learning styles:

Step 5: It is time to teach the correct definitions. Call on students to share a word and their best guess definition. Ask students to explain their thinking as they share why they guessed a certain definition. This is a great time to point kids back to the video or re-teach parts of the demonstration to give context clues. Students may notice word parts that are related to words they know. Use this understanding to explain the new word. Go through the list as a class, calling on prior knowledge to discuss each word. (Tip: If necessary for increasing engagement, draw names from a jar and return them each time, so that everyone has the possibility of being called every time.)

Step 6: You now have your vocabulary list, complete with correct definitions and connections to prior knowledge. You can add to it as you engage in future hands-on lab work, and you can add unfamiliar terms from the reading as well.

Part 1: Integrated Vocabulary

Step 7: Use your vocabulary list throughout the rest of this unit as you move through steps 2-4 of the vocabulary program.

Student Perspective: "When I create the list myself, it becomes more relevant and easier to assimilate into other classroom activities and assignments."

Tip: You may find it helpful to provide your students with a word list and a chart for them to fill in during lab activities. See the example below from an electrical construction class.

Common Core Connection

- Determine meanings of domain-specific words in context CCSS.ELA-LITERACY.RST.11-12.4
- Work toward proficient independent understanding of text CCSS.ELA-LITERACY.RST.11-12.10

Electrical Wiring Overview

Vocabulary for Chapter 1, "Residential Workplace Safety"

Read the terms for Chapter 1 and put each word into one of the 3 columns below.

> Ampere, Arc, Arc-blast, Arc-flash, Circuit Conductor, Double insulated, Electrical shock, Grounding, GFCI, Hazard Insulator Load, National Electrical Code, OSHA, Ohm, Ohm's Law, PPE (personal protective equipment), Polarized plug, Power source, Resistance, SDS (safety data sheet), Scaffold, Shall, Ventricular Fibrillation, Volt, Voltage

WORDS I KNOW—100%	WORDS I THINK I KNOW	WORDS I NEED MORE HELP WITH

21

Student-Led Word List (reading version)

Gist: Students create their own vocabulary lists, connect the words to their prior knowledge, and use them in speaking and writing.

When to use: During in-class reading, to integrate vocabulary learning. At the beginning of a new unit to introduce new vocabulary.

How It Works

Step 1: Select a complex text for your students to read. This is a great opportunity for CTE teachers to introduce professional materials, manuals, and journal articles from your field. (See page 201 for what makes text "complex"). You may also chart like the one on page 21.

Step 2: Say, "Before we read, skim the text and pick out 5-10 words that seem unfamiliar or difficult. Even if you know all the words, write down the 5 that are hardest to explain. This isn't a test, and it's not for a grade—we just need to decide together which words to learn." You may also want to encourage students to annotate as they read, in order to practice critical reading. We have included an annotation system at the end of this activity.

Step 3: Read the text silently or in pairs. (You can use the paired reading strategy on page 104 in conjunction with this one. Once you are comfortable with this style of teaching vocabulary, you can even chunk the reading and combine this vocabulary reading with the Specified Summary reading on page 22. Writing summaries will teach students to zero in on the meaning of unfamiliar words using context clues.)

Step 4: Say, "Now, write your best guess or explanation of the terms you've picked. Sometimes writing it down helps us to figure out the meaning, and other times it shows us that a word we thought was familiar is a little harder to explain than we thought." Allow a few minutes for this step. TIP: Be sure to have students write their names on this and turn them in at the end of class, so you can use them to get a better understanding of prior knowledge.

The Why

As quick as: 20 minutes

Multiple learning styles:

Step 5: It is time to teach the correct definitions. Call on students to share a word and their best guess definition. Ask students to explain their thinking as they share why they guessed a certain definition. This is a great time to point kids back toward the text to look for context clues. They often notice word parts that are related to words they know. Use this understanding to explain the new word. Go through the list as a class, calling on prior knowledge to discuss each word. (Tip: If necessary for increasing

engagement, draw names from a jar and return them each time, so that everyone has the possibility of being called every time.)

Step 6: You now have your vocabulary list, complete with correct definitions and connections to prior knowledge. You can add to it as you encounter additional texts or other information.

Step 7: Use your vocabulary list throughout the rest of this unit as you move through steps 2-4 of the vocabulary program.

Student Perspective: "When I create the list myself, it becomes more relevant and easier to assimilate into other classroom activities and assignments."

Common Core Connection

- Determine meanings of domain-specific words in context
  CCSS.ELA-LITERACY.RST.11-12.4
- Work toward proficient independent understanding of text
  CCSS.ELA-LITERACY.RST.11-12.10

Annotation System

Gist: A classroom-wide system for annotating text.

When to use: When students to get comfortable with deconstructing text and identifying unfamiliar terms. Don't simply tell them to "read and annotate" without giving them a process for doing so.

The Why

As quick as: 5 minutes

Multiple learning styles:

How It Works

Step 1: Create a key, like the one shown on the facing page, for understanding symbols students can use during annotation. Or have students create it as a group.

Step 2: Each time students read, remind them to annotate, using the symbols from the annotation guide.

Step 3: Encourage students to use their annotation symbols as a guide for discussion. You might say, "Turn to your partner and compare passages that you marked with a question mark."

Common Core Connection

- Determine meanings of domain-specific words and symbols in context
  CCSS.ELA-LITERACY.RST.11-12.4
- Sort ideas into categories
  CCSS.ELA-LITERACY.RST.11-12.5
- Work toward proficient independent understanding of text
  CCSS.ELA-LITERACY.RST.11-12.10

Annotation Key

? = Ask a question, something that puzzles you

"The text mentions a DNA study. What does DNA stand for?"

!!! = Note an interesting or very important phrase or paragraph

"I didn't realize that tapeworms can grow to 23 meters!"

C = Connection to another text or piece of evidence

"The Ebola virus is like the AIDS virus we read about yesterday because…"

* = Access prior knowledge; I already knew that!

"I knew that photosynthesis requires water."

X = Challenge your own thinking with new information

"I had no idea that Nobel invented dynamite."

Box it/Circle it = Words that you don't know, are repeated, or you just like

"I've read the word ignominious and have no idea what that means—I can barely pronounce it!"

Meaning Prediction Chart

Gist: Students create a chart for predicting word meanings.

When to use: Whenever you have very unfamiliar terms.

The Why

As quick as: 5 minutes

Metacognition (thinking about thinking): Students identify concepts that they can mentally connect to a vocabulary term. They begin to activate prior knowledge and understand how they learn best.

Multiple learning styles:

How It Works

Step 1: Display words one at a time on a screen slideshow or white board. Ask students to write the term in the boxes of the form (sample on the facing page).

Step 2: Say, "Please write the term in the box and then write in pencil what you think the term means. If you are struggling, think about what the term brings to mind. If you really have no idea about the term, then just write a question mark in the box beside the term." It is wise to have them write in pencil so that they can erase if they need to.

Step 3: Give students 1-2 minutes with each slide to predict the term's meaning and write something in the box with the term. Go through each term.

Step 4: Project the first term again and ask students what they thought the definition was. Deliberately probe for the students' thinking, asking what they mentally connected the term to.

Step 5: Lead a discussion of the terms' meanings, making sure that students correct or add to their original definitions. Explain that writing definitions verbatim (word for word) from the text is not helpful for retention. Encourage students to think about how they might be using the term during this unit, creating more of a pretest feel to this activity.

> **Common Core Connection**
> - Determine meanings of domain-specific words in context
>   CCSS.ELA-LITERACY.RST.11-12.4
> - Work toward proficient independent understanding of text
>   CCSS.ELA-LITERACY.RST.11-12.10

Part 1: Integrated Vocabulary

Meaning Prediction Chart

Unit:	
Term: Definition:	Term: Definition:
Term: Definition:	Term: Definition
Term: Definition:	Term: Definition:
Term: Definition:	Term: Definition
Term: Definition:	Term: Definition:
Term: Definition:	Term: Definition

Meaning Prediction through Think-Pair-Share

Gist: Students compare and discuss their predictions about word meaning.

When to use: Before defining terms, to engage students through prediction.

The Why

As quick as: 15 minutes

Metacognition (thinking about thinking): Prediction primes students' brains as they seek to know if they were right. Explain the power of prediction to your students.

Multiple learning styles:

Student perspective: "It feels good to figure out the definitions without being told!"

How It Works

Step 1: Have students write the terms they will study on a chart like the sample on the facing page. Give them 10-12 minutes to quietly reflect on what they think the meaning of each term is and to write it in the center column.

Step 2: Walking the room as students work, help give direction to struggling students.

Step 3: Once students have written their best guesses, partner students and allow another 4-5 minutes for students to compare their predictions and decide who is closer to the best definition.

Step 4: Lead the whole class through each term, clarifying which responses are best and why. Instruct students to write in the far-right column if their first attempt was incorrect. If they were correct, they do not need to rewrite it.

Twist: Replace the chart with Post-it notes, allowing students to physically engage, getting out of their seats and sticking their predictions on the board or the wall. Then, during the final whole-class sharing time, students would choose the best Post-it definition and record it in their notebooks.

Common Core Connection
- Determine meanings of domain-specific words in context CCSS.ELA-LITERACY.RST.11-12.4
- Work toward proficient independent understanding of text CCSS.ELA-LITERACY.RST.11-12.10

Meaning Prediction Chart
for Think-Pair-Share

TERM:	What I THINK it means:	BEST DEFINITION:

Notecard Chunking (Identifying Terms in Context)

Gist: Students listen for terms used in context and determine their definitions during breaks in direct instruction.

When to use: During a discussion, lecture, or demonstration. Can also be used as a formative check for understanding. Great for any CTE class.

The Why

As quick as: 10 minutes, with direct instruction interspersed

Metacognition (thinking about thinking): Ask students to describe their prior knowledge that helped them to define a term. Prompt them to identify how this connection helped them decode the term.

Multiple learning styles:

With CTE terms, students retain vocabulary best if terms are introduced in context, pausing to learn them, rather than frontloading terms as is common for fictional text (Beers & Probst, 2012).

How It Works

Step 1: Plan to chunk direct instruction time to less than 15 minutes.

Step 2: Write on the board a list of 3-10 terms that will be covered during the first section of direct instruction.

Step 3: Instruct students to write one term on each side of each card and to think about how you use the term during the discussion/lecture time.

Step 4: Proceed with chunked direct instruction.

Step 5: After one segment of direct instruction, challenge students to write a definition in their own words for each term covered in that segment.

Step 6: Walk throughout the room as students attempt to write a definition or recall the context in which you used the term.

Step 7: Once students have completed the terms for that segment of instruction, run through each of them to hear what students have written and clear up any misconceptions. Now is a great time for re-teaching and elaborating on a term.

Step 8: Continue the process with the next chunked segment of instruction, until you have finished your entire lesson and covered all terms.

Step 9: Ask students to rubber band their cards save them as a study aid. They can later add to their notecard set and elaborate on their definitions during future discussions.

Twist: Rather than directly asking for student volunteers to share their definitions with the class, pair students to work on the definitions and contexts together as they write.

Part 1: Integrated Vocabulary

Student perspective: "It's easier to pay attention and see the purpose of the vocabulary list when we pause and use notecards."

Common Core Connection
- Determine meanings of domain-specific words in context
CCSS.ELA-LITERACY.RST.11-12.4
- Work toward proficient independent understanding of text
CCSS.ELA-LITERACY.RST.11-12.10

Students save their notecards to use later for studying. Notecards can also be used during discussions, pairing them or challenging students to explain their connection to prior knowledge. As you become more comfortable with notecards, you'll find seemingly endless uses for them.

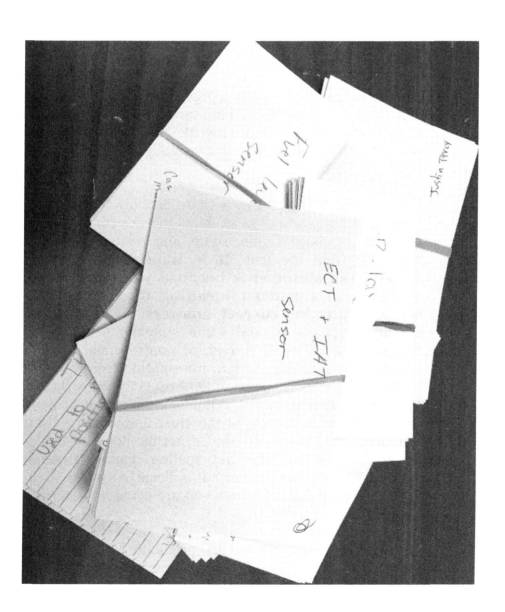

Prediction Guide (Vocabulary Version)

(See Prediction Guide (productive talk version) in part 2. Both adapted from Dr. Mark A. Forget's "Anticipation Guide," Forget, 2004)

Gist: Students read prepared statements rephrased from a text (video, audio presentation) that include uses of new vocabulary terms. Students choose whether they agree or disagree. They discuss and explain their choices, then they read/view/listen and note their correct or incorrect predictions. Afterwards, they discuss again and reach consensus.

When to use: Before and during any reading, viewing, or listening activity, to introduce vocabulary in context and to engage students with prediction. Great for any CTE class.

The Why

As quick as: 30 minutes

Tip: Creating prediction guides takes some work up front, but it pays off in student engagement! Plus, you can save them to re-use each year.

Metacognition (thinking about thinking): Prediction gives a purpose to the reading. When students know this purpose, they begin to understand the process of reading critically.

Multiple learning styles:

How It Works

Step 1 (before class): Create a prediction guide about word meanings from the day's reading assignment, video or audio presentation, or in-class demonstration. You can create an anticipation guide for virtually any "text." Here's how:

Read or watch the text or activity, looking for the most important terms you want students to learn from it. Then, for each of those terms, write one related statement reworded from the text. **It is important that you reword the statements because your goal is for students to construct meaning themselves, not simply hunt for correct answers.** Each statement should be plausible, and some statements should be complex, vague, overly broad, or controversial. Include some statements that contain information from multiple sections of the text, so that students must interpret the text broadly rather than picking out answers. Some statements may be correct, some may be incorrect, and others may not have a correct answer. Vocabulary terms should be bolded or underlined on the anticipation guide. Example statement (construction class): It is illegal in the U.S. to call yourself an ***architect*** unless you are licensed by a state. (This is true.)

Step 2 (in class): Introduce prediction. Explain that strategic thinkers naturally make predictions and keep their predictions in mind while reading or listening. Emphasize that predictions do not have to be right—either way, they give a purpose for reading and help make it more interesting. In our case, the purpose is to gain a more complete understanding of our vocabulary terms. You may even introduce the idea of prediction by modeling: "I'm betting 75% of you posted to Twitter over the weekend." Then ask for a show of hands and explain how you're much more invested in the answer after having made a prediction.

Step 3: Students read the statements individually and connect each statement to prior knowledge of the vocabulary term, predicting whether the statement will prove to be correct. Students mark "correct" statements with a checkmark.

Step 4: Students connect with an elbow-partner, discussing each person's response to each statement and attempting to reach a consensus by explaining their logic and prior knowledge to each other. The teacher should move around the room, monitoring these discussions and checking for prior knowledge.

Step 5: Students read the text (silently or with their partner), seeking evidence to back up or refute their predictions. For a video or audio presentation, students should watch or listen, making note on their anticipation guide when evidence is given. Students should note all evidence that relates to a statement, even conflicting evidence. Modification: for low-level readers, you may want to group them together and read aloud, reading a statement yourself and then having them read it back to you before discussion.

Step 6: Students return to their partner or a small group to discuss their evidence. Their goal is to reach a consensus about all the statements AND all the logical evidence for their statements.

Common Core Connection
- Cite textual evidence to support analysis
  CCSS.ELA-LITERACY.RST.11-12.1
- Determine meanings of domain-specific words in context
  CCSS.ELA-LITERACY.RST.11-12.4
- Work toward proficient independent understanding of text
  CCSS.ELA-LITERACY.RST.11-12.10

Step 7: Teacher leads a whole-group discussion in which students share and defend the statements they agree with, eventually coming up with an agreed-upon definition for each term. Encourage argument between students, and encourage students to probe into each other's reasoning as they question each other's positions.

Student perspective: "Reading is more interesting when I'm looking to see whether I was right or wrong!"

Making It Work – Introducing Vocabulary

- How can I combine the lab and the classroom while introducing vocabulary terms?

- How can I encourage speaking, writing, reading, and listening while introducing vocabulary terms?

Notes:

VOCABULARY STEP 2: PRACTICE

After introducing vocabulary terms in context, find ways to get students practicing using them and committing them to memory. Try to incorporate vocabulary practice both in the lab and the classroom, in ways that engage multiple learning styles. Get students speaking, writing, and visually representing the terms. To get you started, below are several ways to incorporate vocabulary practice, and the following pages hold more detailed activity suggestions.

Create activities in which students...

- Write step-by-step instructions using vocabulary terms
- Write text for a web page using vocabulary terms
- Explain vocabulary terms to another student
- Create an instructional video using vocabulary terms
- Create with pictures a visual dictionary for the class library (see Career Curator on page 180)
- Perform a demonstration for the class, using vocabulary terms
- Use a specified number of terms in a class discussion (a timed challenge).

Forced Lab Conversation

Gist: Students describe aloud exactly what their classmate is doing, and why, using technical terms.

When to use: During lab work, to give students an opportunity to use and explain vocabulary terms in context. Great for any CTE class.

The Why

As quick as: 5 minutes

Multiple learning styles:

How It Works

Step 1: Group students in threes (or more) during lab work.

Step 2: Say, "Today we will incorporate conversation into our lab work. Take turns doing the [lab activity]. The group members who are not doing the activity will then have a conversation describing what their partner is doing and why."

Step 3: Give students a word bank, or simply specify a number of vocabulary words from their list that they should use during their conversation. You may want to assign one person to keep track of how many vocabulary words have been used by each group member.

Step 4: The conversation should include questions, explanations, and descriptions. Students may feel awkward at first, but having a list of words they are trying to use will make it a fun challenge.

Step 5: After a portion of the activity, have students switch so someone else can perform the lab activity. Continue switching periodically as time allows.

Twist: Have students narrate their lab partner's activity as they make a video.

Student perspective: "I like group challenges, and I understand the words better when I say them out loud."

Common Core Connection
- Follow multi-step procedure and analyze results
  CCSS.ELA-LITERACY.RST.11-12.3
- Determine meanings of domain-specific words in context
  CCSS.ELA-LITERACY.RST.11-12.4
- Synthesize information from text and simulations into a coherent process
  CCSS.ELA-LITERACY.RST.11-12.9
- Work toward proficient independent understanding of text
  CCSS.ELA-LITERACY.RST.11-12.10
- Use technology to produce or publish projects in response to feedback
  CCSS.ELA-LITERACY.WHST.11-12.6

> **Differentiating Talk Time**
>
> Forced Lab Conversation can be as simple and informal as simply reminding lab partners to talk through the steps aloud, or it can be a more formal challenge using a word bank and question prompts.
>
> Think of this exercise as a good opportunity to differentiate instruction. Provide question prompts and word banks for students who may need them (see page 108 for a list of question stems), and challenge others to carry on in conversation for as long as they can without looking at the word bank.

How can I create more opportunities to use vocabulary terms aloud in context?

Notes:

Reflective Dictionary

Originally created by Karen Gillie, a teacher in Fort Wayne, IN

Gist: Students maintain a booklet in which they write one vocabulary term per page, record its definition in their own words, make notes on where they've seen it and any mental connections, and draw a graphic representation of the term.

When to use: Throughout the school year, to practice and reinforce difficult vocabulary terms. See note below on serial position effect. This is a great activity for the last 5-10 minutes of class.

How It Works

Step 1: Create blank booklets using the reproducible template on page 40.

Step 2: Give students time to update their dictionaries throughout the year, and bring them into the lab to connect vocab learning to physical actions. The dictionaries don't necessarily have to include every vocabulary word; instead, you could use them for words the student is unfamiliar with or has struggled with on assessments.

> **Common Core Connection**
> - Summarize complex concepts by paraphrasing
>   CCSS.ELA-LITERACY.RST.11-12.2
> - Determine meanings of domain-specific words in context
>   CCSS.ELA-LITERACY.RST.11-12.4
> - Synthesize information from multiple sources into a coherent understanding
>   CCSS.ELA-LITERACY.RST.11-12.9
> - Work toward proficient independent understanding of text
>   CCSS.ELA-LITERACY.RST.11-12.10

The Why

As quick as: 5 minutes

Metacognition (thinking about thinking): Drawing graphic representations and identifying relevant prior knowledge helps students understand how they learn. Students can engage in good discussion about why they chose a particular visual representation.

Multiple learning styles:

A page from a student's reflective dictionary

Term

In my own words (definition):	Graphic representation (drawing):
What does this remind me of?	
Where have I seen this?	

Term

In my own words (definition):	Graphic representation (drawing):
What does this remind me of?	
Where have I seen this?	

Part 1: Integrated Vocabulary

Serial Position Effect

Studies show that we remember information best when it's presented at the beginning (*primacy*) or end (*recency*) of a sequence, and we forget what we learned in the middle (Myers & DeWall, 2015).

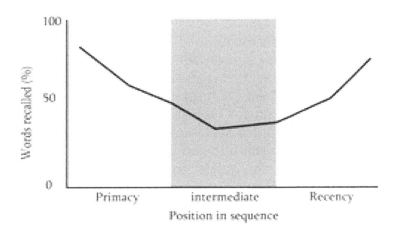

(image source: Wikipedia.org)

Serial position effect applies on a small scale (we remember words and numbers at the beginning and end of a list), and most teachers see evidence that it applies on a large scale too: students remember information taught in the early and late months of the schoolyear, while information in the middle tends to run together. To combat the mid-year slump in retaining information, develop a system that brings previously learned vocabulary and concepts back into students' working memory repeatedly throughout the entire year. Regularly use vocabulary terms from students' reflective dictionaries on entrance & exit cards, in 30-second talkabout sessions, and in prediction brainstorming activities to ensure your students retain the terms you're teaching from October through February. The chart below is a projection of how the serial position effect might create a mid-year slump in vocabulary learning.

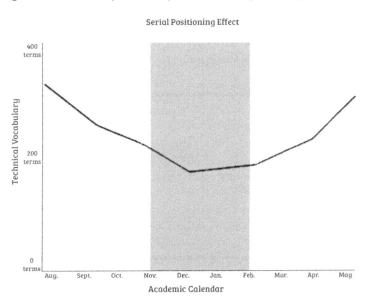

Technology Games

Gist: Check out this list of websites that can reinforce vocabulary learning with variety and fun.

When to use: These games are great for review and formative checks for understanding.

The Why

As quick as: 20 minutes

Students retain the meanings of terms when they make connections and use them in an enjoyable context.

Multiple learning styles:

Quizlet Live – This FREE in-class, team-based learning game gets students working together to match terms and definitions. You'll need at least six students; a computer, tablet, or phone for each student; and 10-20 minutes of class time. Find more information and instructions at https://quizlet.com/features/live.

Tip: Increase the challenge by having students create their own Quizlet Live vocabulary games for the class to play. Scan below for a reproducible version of this assignment.

Kahoot! – This FREE in-class review game is an excellent complement to Quizlet Live. Kahoot allows you to challenge students individually with questions that you design or borrow from another teacher who has already created quizzes on the site. Quizzes can range from a few questions to many, depending on your needs and schedule. Use Kahoot to check for understanding after a lecture, as an alternative to traditional Q&A. Find more information and instructions at https://create.kahoot.it, or scan the code to the right.

Common Core Connection

- Determine meanings of domain-specific words in context
  CCSS.ELA-LITERACY.RST.11-12.4
- Integrate and evaluate information from diverse media formats
  CCSS.ELA-LITERACY.RST.11-12.7
- Work toward proficient independent understanding of text
  CCSS.ELA-LITERACY.RST.11-12.10

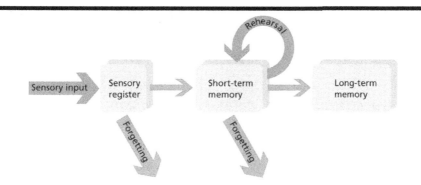

Why Play Games?

Word walls and vocabulary lists alone are never enough. Here's why.
Grab a piece of scrap paper, and draw two large circles. In the first circle—from your memory—complete the "heads" side of the U.S. penny. Which direction does the profile face? What are the words and numbers? Add as much detail as you can recall. When you've drawn all you can, move to the second circle and complete the "tails" side. Finally, pull a penny out of your pocket and check your own memory. How'd you do? Most people cannot draw the penny well, despite having seen a penny thousands of times. We don't pay close attention to a penny's details because the details don't seem to matter.

Students see vocabulary words on lists and review sheets over and over. But that doesn't mean they're paying attention. In vocabulary practice, we must provide 3 key experiences:
1. Require attention to terms and concepts – Simply finding the correct answer for a worksheet does not require students to pay attention and think more deeply about the terms.
2. Rehearse terms and concepts – In the memory diagram above, the blue "rehearsal" arrow is key. Educational researcher Barak Rosenshine found that master teachers consistently spend at least 8 minutes per hour of instruction rehearsing key terms and concepts (Rosenshine, 2012).
3. Provide sensory experiences – Sensory memory is important to the recall stage or memory. When emotions and senses are involved, memory improves.

Short weekly game sessions can help add these key experiences to your vocabulary practice. They demand attention and deep thought, allow teachers to clarify and review, and include laughter and fun.

Two-Column Notes

"When taking notes, some students get bogged down in the details, while others don't write much at all."

Gist: Explicitly teach students a notetaking strategy that helps them practice paraphrasing, deleting, and elaborating on what they hear and see. Engaging in these thinking tasks as they read or listen gets them thinking more deeply.

When to use: teach this strategy early in the year, and reinforce it periodically by having students use it during direct instruction.

The Why

As quick as: 5 minutes added to any lesson

Metacognition (thinking about thinking): Learning to organize information helps students see how ideas interact. They learn to create an outline of their own reading and thinking processes.

Multiple learning styles:

How It Works

Step 1: Have students draw a vertical line a couple of inches from the left margin of their paper, and a horizontal line a few inches from the bottom.

Step 2: Say, "The narrow column is for key points, vocabulary terms, or essential questions. The wider section is for paraphrasing and recording important details about the items on the left side. The space at the bottom is for writing a summary at the end."

Step 3: Encourage students not to use full sentences or write directly from the text. Explain that images are acceptable, too. The purpose is to record what matters, in terms they will be able to understand later. (Continued on next page.)

Step 4: Begin using text, video, or performance to allow students to practice notetaking with this structure. Provide a few minutes at the end for students to summarize at the bottom of each page.

Step 5: Get students using their notes. Check out the suggestions on the facing page for some ideas.

Check out this helpful video by Sofia Tree Productions about using 2-column notes to stress vocabulary terms, essential questions, and central ideas with supporting details. Scan the QR code to watch.
https://www.youtube.com/watch?v=w3pM5hEgBk4

Part 1: Integrated Vocabulary

Get students using their notes!

A few ideas:
1. Create a writing assignment in which students must compare or contrast main ideas from their notes, without looking back at the primary source.
2. Assign a 30-second "micro-presentation," in which students stand and summarize one key point from their notes.
3. Pair students up to combine their individual notes into a summary together.
4. Encourage them to use their notes during review games.

Student perspective: "I never used my notes before, but now I take notes I can actually use!"

Allied health careers teacher Lisa Schaefer has scaffolded instruction for one student by providing two-column notes with some categories and page numbers already listed on the left side. Later, the student will be expected to take two-column notes without scaffolding.

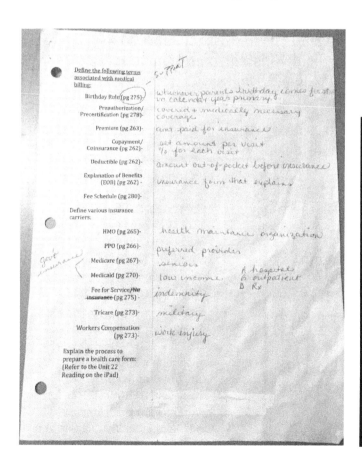

Common Core Connection

- Cite textual evidence, attend to distinctions and inconsistencies
  CCSS.ELA-LITERACY.RST.11-12.1
- Determine central ideas, summarize concepts, paraphrase
  CCSS.ELA-LITERACY.RST.11-12.2
- Determine meanings of domain-specific words in context
  CCSS.ELA-LITERACY.RST.11-12.4
- Analyze text structure into categories or hierarchies
  CCSS.ELA-LITERACY.RST.11-12.5
- Work toward proficient independent understanding of text
  CCSS.ELA-LITERACY.RST.11-12.10

Nine Diamond Organizer

Gist: Students prioritize a list of nine terms (or pictures representing them) in order of importance or relevance to a topic.

When to use: To get students thinking more deeply about terms they have learned, and to get them comfortable with speaking about those terms.

The Why

As quick as: 15 minutes

Metacognition (thinking about thinking): Explaining their ranking process gives students the opportunity to see their own thought process.

Multiple learning styles:

How It Works

Step 1: Copy and distribute the graphic organizer on the following page, or choose to have students make their own large version on chart paper or with Post-it notes.

Step 2: List terms to be ordered on the board. You can also list phrases or steps in a process, being sure to include several vocabulary terms. It is not necessary for there to be one correct answer of a ranking.

Step 3: Group students to work together, so they'll have to come to agreement. This will force them to speak the terms out loud, which helps them learn.

Step 4: Say, "As a group, choose the most important term or phrase, and write it in the top of the diamond. Then write the least important at the bottom of the diamond. Place the two next most important and two next least important near the top and bottom respectively, with the three remaining in the middle."

Step 4: Facilitate as students rank terms or phrases. Remember, the usefulness of this activity does not depend on there being one correct answer. If there is ambiguity, students learn nuances of terms and phrases as they discuss.

Step 5. Compare the rankings of the class, asking each group to explain their choices with evidence from text or in-class learning.

Student Perspective: "I really like when we get out of our seats and create an organizer on the wall with Post-its. It's easier for me to get interested that way."

Common Core Connection

- Cite textual evidence, attend to distinctions and inconsistencies CCSS.ELA-LITERACY.RST.11-12.1
- Determine central ideas, summarize concepts, paraphrase CCSS.ELA-LITERACY.RST.11-12.2
- Determine meanings of domain-specific words in context CCSS.ELA-LITERACY.RST.11-12.4
- Analyze text structure into categories or hierarchies CCSS.ELA-LITERACY.RST.11-12.5
- Work toward proficient independent understanding of text CCSS.ELA-LITERACY.RST.11-12.10

Part 1: Integrated Vocabulary

 To see a video of the nine diamond organizer in action, scan this QR code.

Nine Diamond Organizer

Making It Work – Practicing Vocabulary

- How can I combine the lab and the classroom while practicing vocabulary terms?

- How can I encourage speaking, writing, reading, and listening while practicing vocabulary terms?

Notes:

VOCABULARY STEP 3: EXPLORE RELATIONSHIPS

After introduction and practice, help students to develop a more complex understanding of vocabulary words by thinking about how they relate to one another. You can do this informally, by calling attention to it during class discussions about your content area. You can also add specific activities for this purpose. Graphic organizers are especially helpful for defining word relationships. With a little creative thinking, almost any graphic organizer that you already use for problem-solving or discussion can become a tool to emphasize vocabulary terms. The following pages include activities and several diagrams of graphic organizers for exploring word relationships.

Affinity Diagram (Categorizing Words)

"I need my students to practice their vocabulary more, but drill and practice routines get boring."

Gist: Students analyze a list of random vocabulary terms, where some terms are overarching concepts and others are attributes, details, or examples. Students determine which terms fit into each category.

When to use: to replace traditional vocabulary drill and practice. Great as a pause to break up direct instruction. Use this organizer as a competitive timed activity or a cooperative challenge.

The Why

As quick as: 5 minutes

Metacognition (thinking about thinking): Categorizing words helps students see the big picture of how they understand concepts. It adds dimension to a student's understanding of a word's meaning.

Multiple learning styles:

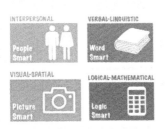

How It Works

Step 1: Distribute one of the graphic organizers on the following pages. Then distribute (or project on a screen) a list of random vocabulary terms in which some are overarching concepts and others are attributes, details, or examples.

Step 2: Say, "Your task will be to organize the terms into categories that show the relationships between them. I will set a timer for _ minutes."

Step 3: Set timer and let students begin thinking and filling out the organizer.

Step 4: Facilitate as students work to organize the terms, tracking their progress (mentally or with checklist) and noting which students struggle with finding relationships between the terms.

Step 5: Follow a think-pair-share method. When time is up, students can turn and share their answers with another student. Then pull responses as a whole class and model the correct responses on the board. Give supporting examples and pull examples from students on how they thought through the word relationships.

Step 6: Discuss any thinking errors that occurred. For instance, if a student could not think of which terms were the overarching categories, go over them together. Encourage students to consider where there might be gaps in their own learning. Remember to probe for their reasoning. Even if they answered incorrectly, it is important to understand the thinking process behind their answer and discuss whether there may be more than one way to connect the terms.

Twist: Once you have shared aloud as a class and made sure all students understand, have them each write short reflections at the bottom of the organizer page about how the terms are related.

Twist 2: Use the Affinity Diagram to construct a unit overview. Challenge small groups of students to think of the big picture of the unit you're working on, and to come up with three categories or headings they would use if they were going to explain the unit to someone or write a summary on it. They should write the headings or categories in the larger boxes. In the smaller boxes to the right, they should then list vocabulary terms that best fit into each heading. Afterwards, challenge the groups to explain why certain terms fit into the categories where they placed them. Being able to break the main unit topic into categories and then determine which content belongs in each category is an important skill for preparing to write. If you wish, you could then turn this into a writing assignment, challenging students to write a summary that includes their three headings, or to write a more detailed explanation of one of those headings.

Common Core Connection

- Cite textual evidence, attend to distinctions and inconsistencies
  CCSS.ELA-LITERACY.RST.11-12.1
- Determine central ideas, summarize concepts, paraphrase
  CCSS.ELA-LITERACY.RST.11-12.2
- Determine meanings of domain-specific words in context
  CCSS.ELA-LITERACY.RST.11-12.4
- Analyze text structure into categories or hierarchies
  CCSS.ELA-LITERACY.RST.11-12.5
- Work toward proficient independent understanding of text
  CCSS.ELA-LITERACY.RST.11-12.10

Affinity Diagram

Purpose:
To group ideas into categories or themes.

Procedure:
Record the results of a brainstorm by placing an organizing theme or heading in the larger boxes. Write similar concepts or items to the side of each theme or heading.

Part 1: Integrated Vocabulary

Affinity Diagram 2

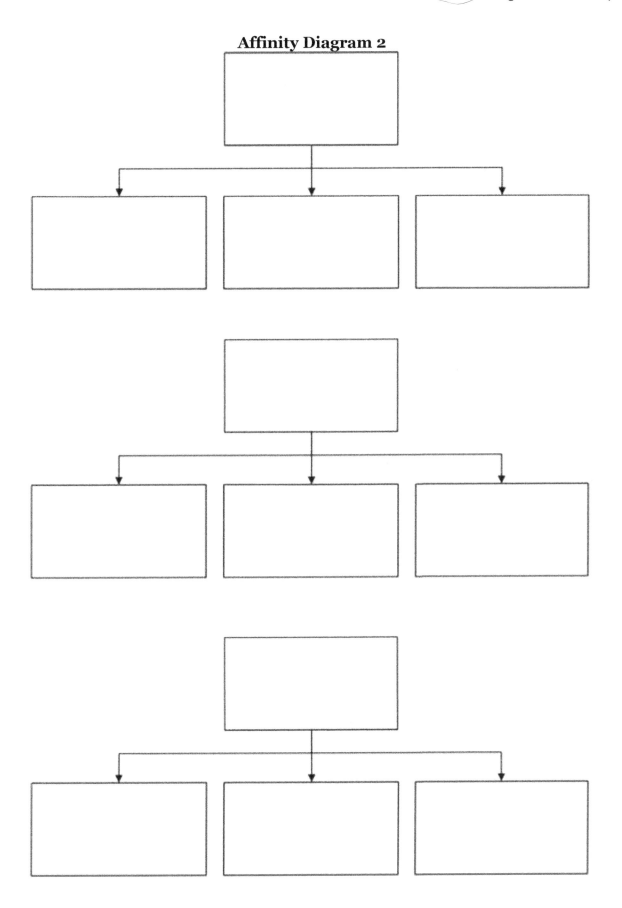

Cause-Effect Chart (Determining Word Relationships)

Gist: Students diagnose a realistic problem by pulling out key terms from text as they read, placing them in a chart to show terms that lead to other terms.

When to use: During reading, or when diagnosing problems or prompting students to think in terms of cause and effect. Great for CTE classes that teach troubleshooting, including automotive classes and health careers.

The Why

As quick as: 5 minutes

Multiple learning styles:

How It Works

Step 1: Present a situation or problem for students to diagnose, along with text or a video segment that will describe several possible causes of the effect you are discussing.

Step 2: Give students one of the graphic organizers on the next two pages, and have them write the problem or situation being diagnosed in the single box to the right, under the heading "effect." For example, in an automotive class, if the problem was that a client said, "My car hesitates," they would write the client's statement in the "effect" box.

Step 3: Tell students the purpose of their reading or viewing: to identify all the causes of the problem.

Step 4: Allow students time to read quietly for the different causes that connect to this effect. During their reading, they should circle or jot down relevant vocabulary terms as they read them in context. Instruct them to use specific vocabulary words in the chart.

Step 5: Have students write possible causes in the left-hand column until they have identified 3 or 4.

Step 6: Instruct students to go back and look at what they wrote down. They should then look back at their circled (or listed) associated vocabulary terms. Any terms that are associated with one of the "possible causes" should be written into the diagram at this point.

Step 7: Bring the class together to discuss the causes and clarify mistakes that they may have made while working on this.

Twist: Once the causes have been discussed, you could quickly partner students and have them rank the causes in order of strongest-to-weakest or most likely. This would require them to get back into the text and look for evidence that some possible causes are more likely than others. Any time students are ranking and justifying, you are pushing them toward more critical, strategic thinking.

Twist 2: Use a cause-effect chart to depict a process. If your vocabulary word describes a process or a result, challenge students to write it in the large box and then use the smaller boxes to describe the necessary steps for producing it. For example, in a culinary class, the word "remouillage" could go in the large box, and a student would write in the smaller boxes the steps for making a remouillage ("After making stock, drain and re-use the bones. Add a fresh sachet of spices. Add a fresh mirepoix of 50% onions, 25% carrots, and 25% celery. Add water to cover. Simmer 4-5 hours. Use to make glazes.")

A lab challenge prepared for auto class. Students will use clipboards to create a cause and effect chart in the lab.

Common Core Connection

- Cite textual evidence, attend to distinctions and inconsistencies
  CCSS.ELA-LITERACY.RST.11-12.1
- Determine central ideas, summarize concepts, paraphrase
  CCSS.ELA-LITERACY.RST.11-12.2
- Determine meanings of domain-specific words in context
  CCSS.ELA-LITERACY.RST.11-12.4
- Analyze text structure into categories or hierarchies
  CCSS.ELA-LITERACY.RST.11-12.5
- Work toward proficient independent understanding of text
  CCSS.ELA-LITERACY.RST.11-12.10

Cause and Effect 1

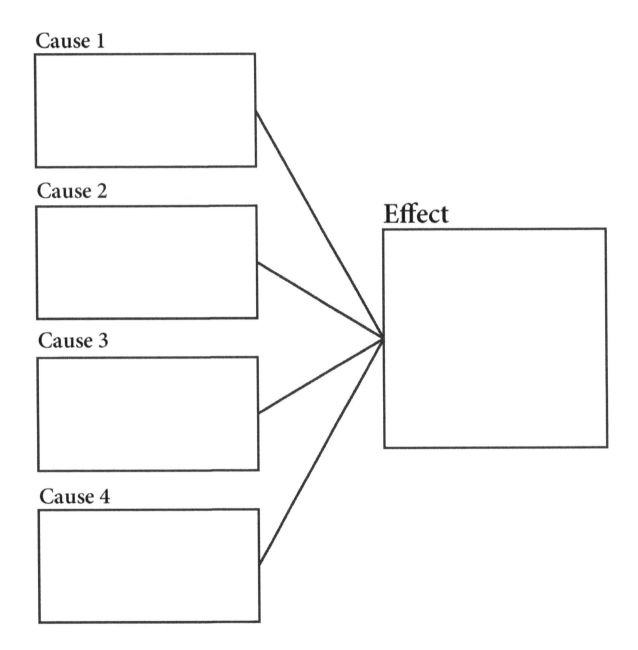

Cause and Effect 2

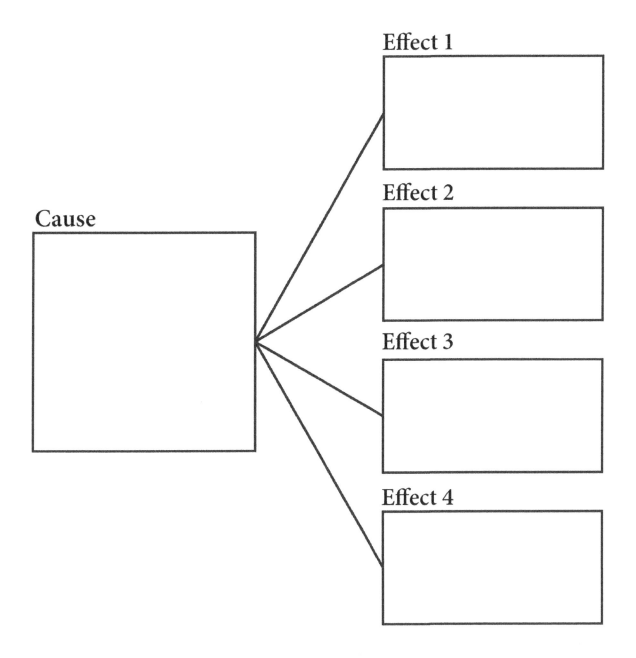

Refine and Define Chart (Writing Concise Definitions)

Gist: Students use the following organizer to help them write term definitions in their own words, honing their thinking and their writing.

When to use: To practice writing skills while reinforcing vocabulary understanding. Great for classes that use complex terminology, such as health careers.

The Why

As quick as: 5 minutes

Multiple learning styles:

How It Works

Step 1: Begin with a vocabulary word or other technical term.

Step 2: Challenge students to write a concise definition of the term that is easy to explain to someone who is unfamiliar with your class. They will use the 5 steps of the chart to hone their definition.

Step 3: First, they write the word, and then its dictionary definition (or a technical definition from the text).

Step 4: In the next box, they choose one word or phrase in the dictionary definition to put in their own words, and write their new version of the definition.

Step 5: They continue this process for the rest of the 5 boxes, refining the definition until it is completely in their own words. You could do this activity as a class, in small groups, or individually.

Twist: Have students think of uses in context, writing situations in which they would use the word.

Common Core Connection

- Determine central ideas, summarize concepts, paraphrase
  CCSS.ELA-LITERACY.RST.11-12.2
- Determine meanings of domain-specific words in context
  CCSS.ELA-LITERACY.RST.11-12.4
- Organize complex information so that each new element builds on that which precedes it
  CCSS.ELA-LITERACY.WHST.11-12.2A
- Produce clear and coherent writing
  CCSS.ELA-LITERACY.WHST.11-12.4
- Develop and strengthen writing by planning, revising, editing, rewriting
  CCSS.ELA-LITERACY.WHST.11-12.5

Refine and Define

Word:
Textbook Definition:

In my own words...

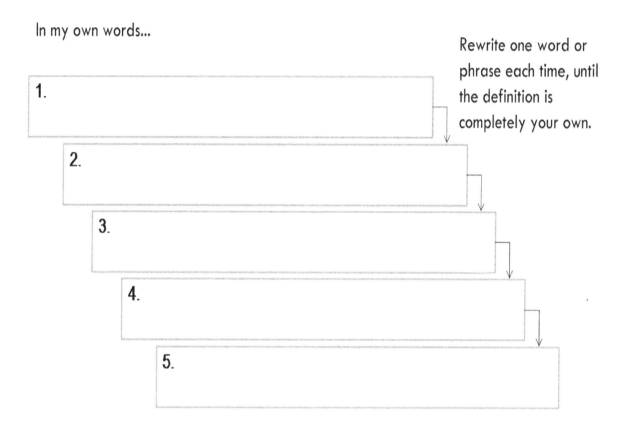

Rewrite one word or phrase each time, until the definition is completely your own.

1.
2.
3.
4.
5.

Flow Chart for Vocabulary Process Terms

Gist: Students put terms in sequential order to show a big-picture understanding of how they fit together.

When to use: When you have several vocabulary terms that all relate to the same process.

The Why

As quick as: 10 minutes

Multiple learning styles:

How It Works

Step 1: Create a word bank of terms that students will put in sequential order. We find it more challenging and fun for students if you put in several extra words, beyond those required, so they must choose which ones are part of the process. Example: For an engine fundamentals class, you might use "intake valve," "exhaust valve," "power stroke," "fuel-air mixture," and so on.

Step 2: Instruct students to fill in one of the flow charts on the following pages (or create one themselves), placing all the terms in sequential order. To engage students kinesthetically, have them create a large flow chart on the floor or wall.

Step 3: Once the chart is filled in with the terms, say, "Now we want to be able to look at this chart and be able to read it smoothly. Turn each step in the chart into a complete sentence that explains the process, using the terms in the chart." Example: "Intake valve ---> fuel-air mixture" becomes "The intake valve opens to allow in fuel-air mixture."

Step 4: Repeat step three with each segment of the flow chart, so the student ends up with a few complete sentences that explain the process smoothly.

Common Core Connection

- Summarize processes, paraphrase
  CCSS.ELA-LITERACY.RST.11-12.2
- Determine meanings of domain-specific words in context
  CCSS.ELA-LITERACY.RST.11-12.4
- Work toward proficient independent understanding of text
  CCSS.ELA-LITERACY.RST.11-12.10
- Write explanatory texts, narrate technical processes
  CCSS.ELA-LITERACY.WHST.11-12.2
- Organize complex information so that each new element builds on that which precedes it
  CCSS.ELA-LITERACY.WHST.11-12.2A
- Use precise language and domain-specific vocabulary
  CCSS.ELA-LITERACY.WHST.11-12.2D
- Develop and strengthen writing by planning and using a new approach
  CCSS.ELA-LITERACY.WHST.11-12.5

Linear Flow Chart

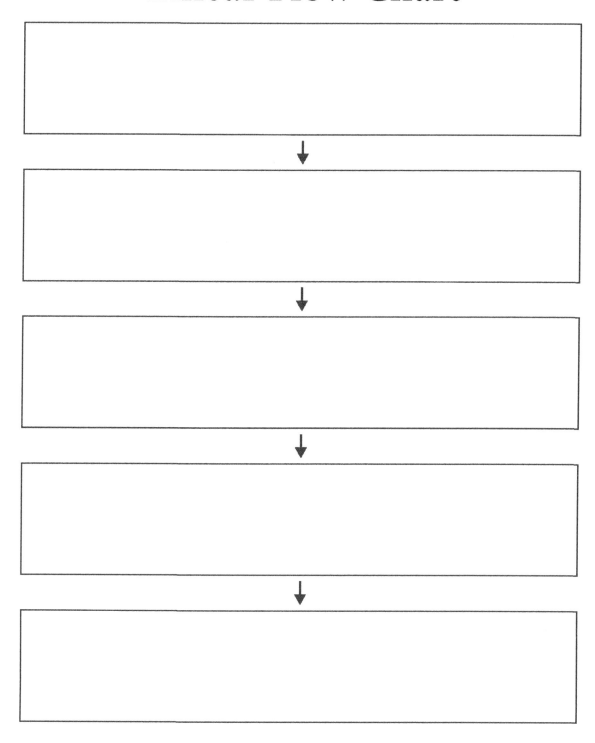

Cyclical Flow Chart

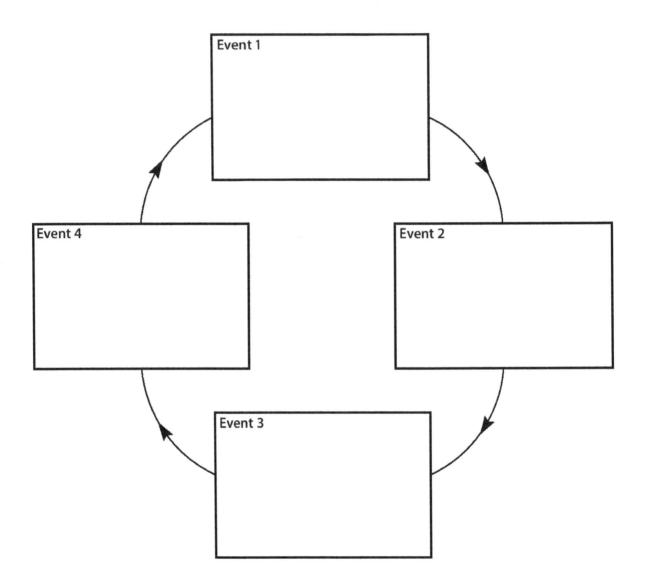

Part 1: Integrated Vocabulary

Cyclical Flow Chart

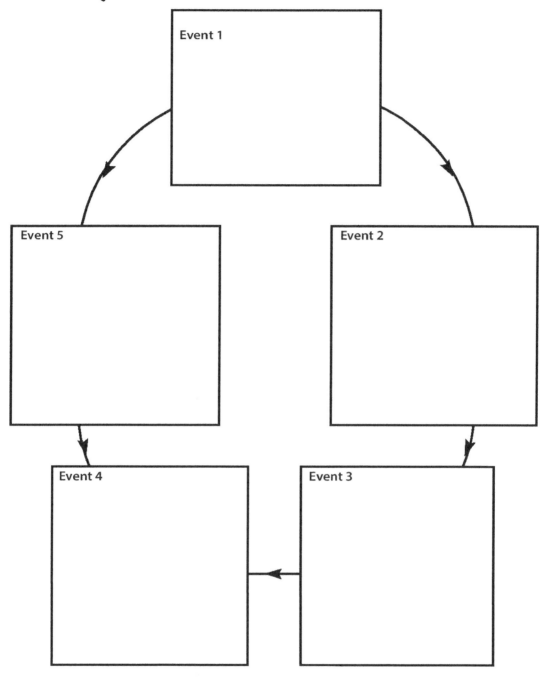

63

Word Tree

Gist: Students group words together based on their relationships and figure out the meaning of the root word.

When to use: With vocabulary words that are related in some way. Great for medical terms in cosmetology and health careers.

The Why

As quick as: 10 minutes

Multiple learning styles:

How It Works

Step 1: Find a word root, prefix, or suffix that is related to some of your vocabulary words (this is especially useful for medical words). Place the root/prefix/suffix into the first box on the word tree shown on the next page.

Step 2: Challenge students to come up with words that are related to the root/prefix/suffix and place them in the "branches" of the tree. For example, if you wrote the root "-alges/algia," students might write "analgesic," "abdominalgia," "adenalgia," "erythromelalgia," and "fibromyalgia." Encourage them to include related words from their prior knowledge that are not necessarily part of your vocabulary list.

Step 3: As a class, have students explain the meanings of any of their "branch" words, if they can.

Step 4: Challenge students to define the meaning of the root/prefix/suffix, based on the meanings of the related words.

Common Core Connection

- Determine meanings of domain-specific words in context
  CCSS.ELA-LITERACY.RST.11-12.4
- Work toward proficient independent understanding of text
  CCSS.ELA-LITERACY.RST.11-12.10
- Use precise language and domain-specific vocabulary
  CCSS.ELA-LITERACY.WHST.11-12.2D

Tips:

- *For planning this activity, you may find it helpful to use visuwords.com, which creates a visual diagram of word relationships.*
- *With any graphic organizer, try having students create their own large version on chart paper or using Post-it notes on the wall. These changes will encourage collaboration and engage bodily-kinesthetic learners.*

Part 1: Integrated Vocabulary

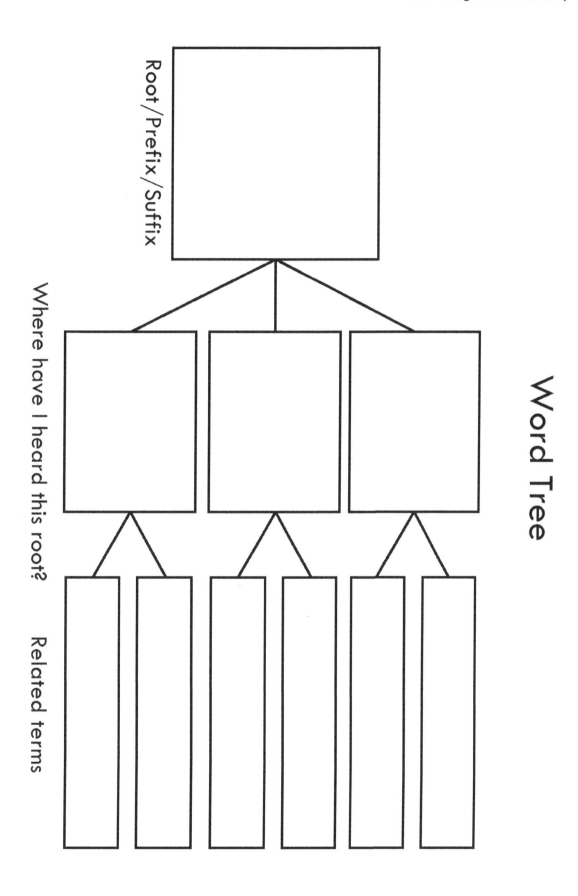

Word Map (Identifying Attributes of Terms)

Gist: Students group terms, list examples, or identify attributes using a graphic organizer.

When to use: With vocabulary words that are part of a category or group, or for vocabulary words that require lots of examples in order to understand them.

The Why

As quick as: 5 minutes

Multiple learning styles:

How It Works

Step 1: Place a vocabulary word in the center box.

Step 2: Challenge students to fill each connecting box with a different example of something that describes or exemplifies the word. For example, if the vocabulary word in your cosmetology class is "antioxidant," the surrounding boxes might be filled with example words such as "Vitamin E," "Vitamin C," "Resveratrol," and "Retinol."

Step 3: Challenge students to write a short definition of each of their example words, or perhaps to list products in which those ingredients are found.

> **Tip:** With any graphic organizer, try having students create their own large version on chart paper or using Post-it notes on the wall. These changes will encourage collaboration and engage bodily-kinesthetic learners.

Common Core Connection

- Summarize information, paraphrase
  CCSS.ELA-LITERACY.RST.11-12.2
- Determine meanings of domain-specific words in context
  CCSS.ELA-LITERACY.RST.11-12.4
- Analyze how information is structured into categories
  CCSS.ELA-LITERACY.RST.11-12.5
- Synthesize information from a range of sources into a coherent understanding of a concept
  CCSS.ELA-LITERACY.RST.11-12.9
- Work toward proficient independent understanding of text
  CCSS.ELA-LITERACY.RST.11-12.10
- Use precise language and domain-specific vocabulary
  CCSS.ELA-LITERACY.WHST.11-12.2D

Part 1: Integrated Vocabulary

Word Maps

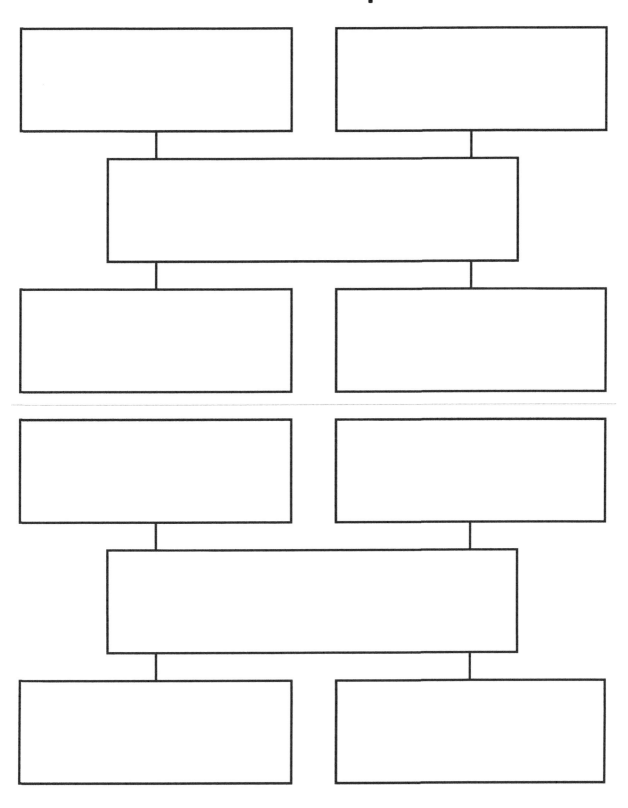

67

Connected Categories

Gist: A game a bit like Apples to Apples, in which students must find a way to connect a previously learned term with a random term from the current lesson.

When to use: To help students connect new learning to previously learned information. Also as test preparation, when terms have been covered but students need to practice using them and find a way to make them stick.

The Why

As quick as: 30 minutes

Multiple learning styles:

How It Works

Step 1 (before class): Write several previously learned vocabulary terms on a set of notecards. Then create a second set of notecards, this time listing terms the students are learning currently. (Scaffolding Note: If you are emphasizing the *definition* of the terms, include the definitions on the back of the cards, or just be sure to discuss each definition during play.)

In an early childhood education class, students are currently learning about child development theorists. The goal today is to help them connect specific theorists' ideas to previously learned topics.

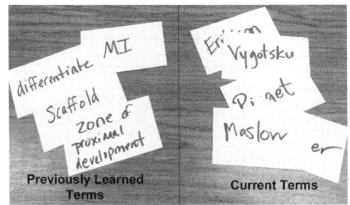

Step 2: Divide the class physically in two halves, with half your students on one side of the room, and half on the other.

Step 3: Distribute one set of cards to each group of students.

Step 4: To play the game, one student from each group comes to the center and brings two cards. In the center of the room you will have a pair of students holding two previously learned terms and two current terms.

Step 5: The two students must work together to connect one of the previously learned terms with one of the current terms. They must say or write a sentence that makes the connection.

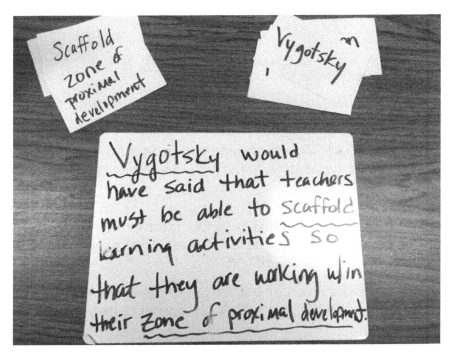

Small whiteboards come in handy for connecting the terms in sentence form. In the early childhood class, the terms "Vygotsky" and "scaffold" can be connected in the sentence above. This particular sentence includes a third term, "zone of proximal development." Bonus points!

Step 6. The rest of the students give a thumbs-up if the sentence makes sense or creates a memorable way to understand the new term. Majority rules. If most thumbs are up, the two students who made the connection each get a point.

Step 7. Remind students during play that this game is not about placing the word itself into its proper category. Instead, it is about finding a clever way to connect what they've learned in one category to what they've learned in another.

Student perspective: "This game is a real challenge, but it's fun! Using the new terms in a sentence about something I already know helps me remember it."

Common Core Connection

- Summarize processes, paraphrase
  CCSS.ELA-LITERACY.RST.11-12.2
- Determine meanings of domain-specific words in context
  CCSS.ELA-LITERACY.RST.11-12.4
- Synthesize information from a range of sources
  CCSS.ELA-LITERACY.RST.11-12.9
- Work toward proficient independent understanding of text
  CCSS.ELA-LITERACY.RST.11-12.10
- Use precise language and domain-specific vocabulary
  CCSS.ELA-LITERACY.WHST.11-12.2D

CTE Vocabulary Grid

(Adapted from a version by Pamela Lopez, Curriculum Specialist at Miami-Dade Public Schools)

Gist: Students record vocabulary terms in categories as they read technical text or work in the lab.

When to use: During reading of manuals, software, or other text. Or bring into the lab with clipboards.

The Why

As quick as: 15 minutes

Encourages analytical skills during the reading of instructional manuals, operating software, or other CTE-related text.

Multiple learning styles:

Step 1: Chunk the text into (X) number of groups, and group your students into (X) number of groups. Assign each group a portion of text.

Step 2: Before reading begins, call students' attention to the categories on the grid so they know what to look for as they read:

Describes software or machinery

Indicates an action

Describes steps of operation

Indicates ways to use software or machinery

Predicts a successful ending of use of software or machinery

Describes troubleshooting actions

Step 3: Each student group reads their portion of text, filling in their grid together. Provide groups with a means of looking up definitions during this time.

Step 4: There may be overlap or ambiguity about which category a term fits into. Encourage students to discuss this ambiguity. If they can articulate a reason why the term fits into more than one category, they should write it in both. The key is to get them to articulate their reasoning, not just to get it correct.

Twist: With students divided into 6 groups, assign each group a separate category and instruct them to fill in as many words/phrases as possible for that one box. Then have each group share their results with the class.

TIP: Scaffold for students who need additional support by giving them a copy of the chart that already has some words or phrases listed. For students needing the highest level of support, consider providing the words and phrases already filled in, and have them point them out as they read them.

Part 1: Integrated Vocabulary

Common Core Connection

- Determine meanings of domain-specific words in context
  CCSS.ELA-LITERACY.RST.11-12.4
- Analyze how text structures information into categories
  CCSS.ELA-LITERACY.RST.11-12.5
- Work toward proficient independent understanding of text
  CCSS.ELA-LITERACY.RST.11-12.10
- Use precise language and domain-specific vocabulary
  CCSS.ELA-LITERACY.WHST.11-12.2D

Sample CTE Vocabulary Grid

Welding Class

Students can construct meaning for themselves as they read and decide into which category a term fits. In this example, a welding teacher purposely separated "terms pertaining to MIG welding" and "terms pertaining to GMAW" so that students would notice which terms overlap.

Welding Vocabulary Overview

Directions: Take the list of terms and apply each to as many of the squares below as you can. Be sure to think through this carefully because some terms will go into multiple boxes.

Terms pertaining to MIG Welding	Terms pertaining to TIG Welding	Terms pertaining to GMAW
GMAW is aka MIG metal inert gas welding	gas-cooled torch gas lens GTAW - tungsten water-cooled torch post flow · CC foot pedal	MIG CO₂ Ar active gas short arc constant potential · spray · pulsed · short-circuit · Globular
Terms pertaining to SMAW	**Terms pertaining to Oxy Fuel Welding**	**Terms specific to Electrical processes**
electrode CC drag welding CV weld bead OCV butt joint primary current secondary current polarity stick welding	acetylene oxygen manifolds pressure regulator oxyacetylene outdated process	electrode CC CV OCV resistance amperage voltage current — primary, secondary CC ? diode

VOCABULARY STEP 4: DEEPEN UNDERSTANDING WITH SWRL

Reinforce vocabulary learning as you go about your daily lessons by incorporating it into Speaking, Writing, Reading, and Listening activities. Some research suggests that a word must be used at least seven times before it is learned, and that that usage must be active (speaking and writing) rather than only passive (reading and listening) (WIDA Consortium, 2012). For an optimal learning environment, "SWRL every day"!

Diagnosing Problems While Performance Testing in the Lab

Gist: Students act out problem-solving aloud as a review on their own while you are performance-testing their peers.

When to use: When you are busy with one-on-one time and cannot direct an activity for the whole class

The Why

As quick as:

Multiple learning styles:

How It Works

Step 1: When you'll be performance testing one student, divide the others into small groups or pairs.

Step 2: Distribute any of the graphic organizers from pages 75-79 . If iPads are available, allow each group to use one for recording a video. Leave a list of vocabulary terms on the board.

Step 3: Say, "In your group, brainstorm some problems that could arise during your performance tests, and record them on the organizer.

Step 4: Say, "Alternating with your partners, act out how you would solve one of the problems, stopping to record your thinking in the chart. Make sure you are speaking up so your partners can hear you. Along the way, your partners should hear you say all the technical vocabulary terms I have written on the board."

Step 5. If you use iPads, have one student per group record a video of the problem-solving steps. Then students should watch themselves on video and critique for professionalism, performance, and correct usage of vocabulary terms.

Common Core Connection

- Follow a complex multi-step procedure and analyze results in terms of text
  CCSS.ELA-LITERACY.RST.11-12.3
- Determine meanings of domain-specific words in context
  CCSS.ELA-LITERACY.RST.11-12.4
- Work toward proficient independent understanding of text
  CCSS.ELA-LITERACY.RST.11-12.10
- Use precise language and domain-specific vocabulary
  CCSS.ELA-LITERACY.WHST.11-12.2D

Part 1: Integrated Vocabulary

Problems/Soultions Chart

What is the problem?	What is the case?	What is the effect?	What are the possible solutions?

Strategies for Solving Problems

Strategy	Advantages	Disadvantages

Part 1: Integrated Vocabulary

What's Your PROBLEM?

Possible Cause #1	**Cause:** What's your evidence? How do you back this claim up? • •
Possible Cause #2	**Cause:** What's your evidence? How do you back this claim up? • •
Possible Cause #3	**Cause:** What's your evidence? How do you back this claim up? • •

Use with "What's Your Problem?" solution organizer on page 78.

What's Your PROBLEM?

Can you support the best possible solution to the problem?

Possible Solution #1	Possible Solution: Evidence to Support 1. 2.
Possible Solution #2	Possible Solution: Evidence to Support 1. 2.
Possible Solution #3	Possible Solution: Evidence to Support 1. 2.

Group Agreement!

Problem Solving Steps

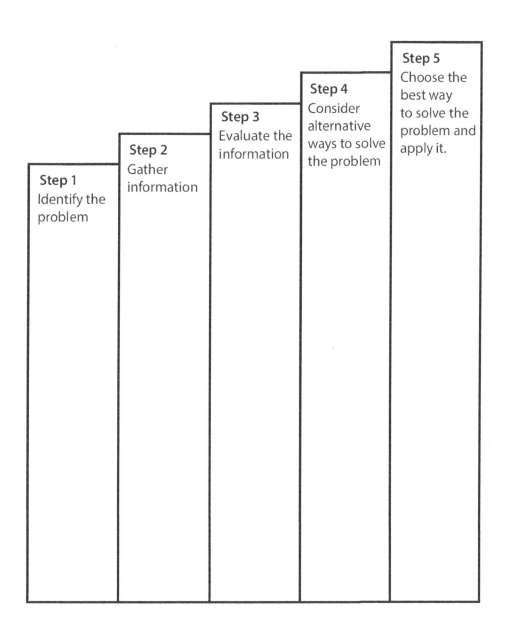

Thirty-Second Talkabout

Gist: Students take turns talking productively about a term for 30 seconds.

When to use: To activate prior knowledge at the beginning of class, to break up direct instruction, or to review at the end of class.

The Why

As quick as: 2 minutes

Multiple learning styles:

Scan this QR code to see a video of the 30-second talkabout in action:

Step 1: Pair students into groups of two.

Step 2: Randomly assign one student in each group the role of "talker" and the other the role of "listener." You can do this quickly by simply saying, "Whoever has a birthday coming sooner is the talker," or something similar.

Step 3: Say, "I'm setting this timer for 30 seconds. The topic is _____ (vocabulary word). Talker, it is your job to keep talking about this topic for 30 seconds without stopping. Listener, your job is to listen and to make sure your partner stays on topic and talks the whole time."

Step 4: Start the timer. Walk throughout the room, listening and assessing your students' understanding of the vocabulary word. Encourage talkers to back up their words with evidence they remember reading from the text. Remember, you can't have a successful talkabout unless you walk about!

Step 5: After the timer goes off, call on various listeners, asking them to share something their partner talked about.

Step 6: Switch! Listeners become talkers, and talkers listen, about a new vocabulary word.

Common Core Connection

- Cite textual evidence
  CCSS.ELA-LITERACY.RST.11-12.1
- Summarize complex concepts by paraphrasing
  CCSS.ELA-LITERACY.RST.11-12.2
- Determine meanings of domain-specific words in context
  CCSS.ELA-LITERACY.RST.11-12.4
- Work toward proficient independent understanding of text
  CCSS.ELA-LITERACY.RST.11-12.10
- Use precise language and domain-specific vocabulary
  CCSS.ELA-LITERACY.WHST.11-12.2D

Twist: Try combining the 30-second talkabout with a graphic organizer: challenge the "talker" to draw a 30-second graphic representation of a concept, while talking about it aloud.

30-Second Simplify

Remember our "simplify" van from page 12? What's so helpful about the 30-second talkabout is that it forces students to internalize complex ideas and create their own meaning so that they can communicate them in a simple, 30-second speech. Complex thought, simple communication.

- Composing a concise verbal explanation for a complex idea leads to real learning. How can you encourage students to use their own words more often?

- What are some other ways you can use short, timed activities to encourage students to simplify complex information, making it their own? Think of short visual representations, multimedia presentations, and physical demonstrations.

Notes:

Entrance and Exit Cards

Gist: Short "bell ringer" question slips that take the place of worksheets and study guides and serve as good accountability measures.

When to use: At the very beginning or end of class, to emphasize technical vocabulary. To deliberately help students focus on key information they will encounter that day. Separates the "nice to know" from the "need to know."

Step 1 (before class): Post a question or problem that is relevant to your topic on the board. Choose a review question that you want to connect to the upcoming class session, or choose an unfamiliar question that will prepare students to think during the upcoming class session. For vocabulary emphasis, make sure your question includes a vocabulary term.

The Why

As quick as: 2 minutes

Multiple learning styles:

Step 2: As students come into class, stand near the doorway and greet them, handing each of them an index card or half-sheet of paper.

Step 3: Say, "Good morning! Please read the question on the board and write your name, and the question on one side of this card, and your response on the other side."

Step 4: Collect the cards after a minute or two as you begin your lesson. Your students will now be primed to think about the day's topic.

Step 5: Look through the cards after class to informally assess your students' understanding. Return the cards to students the next day and encourage them to keep the cards as a study aid.

Twist: Exit Cards - Do the same thing as with entrance cards, but at the end of class to make the most of your time when you have a few extra minutes. If you use it as an Exit card, we recommend asking a question that is directly related to the topic you just covered, or that will pique students' interest for the next day's topic.

Twist 2: If you're looking for ways to eliminate busy work and quizzes, while still assessing students, go through your usual quiz questions and use them as entrance/exit card questions, so you can stop relying on worksheets and quizzes. It will waste less instructional time, and it will provide students with a collection of flashcards to keep as a study aid.

Scan the QR code to the right to access printable entrance/exit cards.

Part 1: Integrated Vocabulary

Common Core Connection

- Summarize complex concepts by paraphrasing
  CCSS.ELA-LITERACY.RST.11-12.2
- Determine meanings of domain-specific words in context
  CCSS.ELA-LITERACY.RST.11-12.4
- Work toward proficient independent understanding of text
  CCSS.ELA-LITERACY.RST.11-12.10
- Use precise language and domain-specific vocabulary
  CCSS.ELA-LITERACY.WHST.11-12.2D

Sample Entrance/Exit Card

Basic Construction Exit Card 1 (E)   Name:_____

```
           15 ft.    10 ft.    20 ft.
        ┌─────────┬──────┬──────────┐
10 ft.  │ kitchen │ den  │          │
        ├─────────┴──────┤  garage  │ 30 ft.
20 ft.  │  living room   │          │
        └────────────────┴──────────┘
              25 ft.        20 ft.
```

1. For the floor plan above, how many feet of crown molding would I need for the entire kitchen and den? _____

2. How many feet larger is the living room than the garage? _____

How did you come up with this number? List the steps you used to think through it—

3. What is the total perimeter of the entire diagram above? _____

4. What is the total perimeter of the entire diagram below? _____

An entrance/exit card can be nothing more than a question from a quiz or review worksheet, like this one to the left. Repurposing questions from quizzes and worksheets is simple and quick to prepare. Eliminate the busywork, and use your time more efficiently.

WebQuest Your Career Path

The Why

As quick as: 30 minutes

Multiple learning styles:

This activity combines digital literacy with productive talk, vocabulary learning, and disciplinary literacy!

Gist: Students create research cards after looking up occupations on the Bureau of Labor Statistics website.

When to use: To more deeply explore occupation vocabulary terms; to incorporate disciplinary literacy, productive talk, digital literacy, and vocabulary learning.

Step 1: List several occupations in your career field as vocabulary terms. Example: In a construction class, your list might look like this:

1. Surveyor
2. Estimator
3. Drafter
4. Superintendent
5. Inspector
6. Planner
7. Expeditor
8. Project Manager
9. Plumber
10. HVAC
11. Electrician

Step 2: Each student should choose 5 occupations to research more deeply. (If you have not yet introduced these terms, consider introducing and practicing with a game to match job titles with basic roles performed.)

Step 3: Introduce the Occupational Outlook Handbook on the Bureau of Labor Statistics website (bls.gov/ooh). Start by showing them how to search, using the search bar at the top right. Each job title has a summary page. Scan here for the search result for "surveyor" from the above list.

Step 4: Here is what a summary looks like for "Surveyor." Go through the example as a class, asking questions so that students can explain the meaning of each line.

2016 Median Pay	$59,390 per year $28.56 per hour
Typical Entry-Level Education	Bachelor's degree
Work Experience in a Related Occupation	Less than 5 years
On-the-job Training	None
Number of Jobs, 2014	44,300
Job Outlook, 2014-24	-2% (Decline)
Employment Change, 2014-24	-900

Step 5: Distribute blank research cards for students to fill out, one card per job title. (Scan here for printable research cards and instructions for navigating the website.) Students should record information about projected job availability, local demand, expected pay, job duties, work environment, and education requirements.

Step 6: After students complete the research cards, have them share what they've learned in groups or pairs. Encourage personal reflection during this discussion. Students should discuss their own possible future career paths, noting what appeals to them and what deters them from a particular career. See the completed research card on the next page as an example.

Step 7: Challenge student groups to create a visual chart or graphic organizer that compares the desirability, income discrepancy, education levels required, or some other data about the jobs they have researched. Scaffolding note: For advanced students, challenge them to choose whatever type of graphic organizer best displays their data. For less advanced students, provide a few styles of organizer to choose from, or have them use one particular type, such as a flow chart depicting the steps to becoming a professional.

Step 8: Have students research local employers they could begin to network with while they are in school.

> *Two Key Questions:*
> 1. How can you begin working toward your best personal career path right now?
> 2. How to people successfully network in this career? How important is it for you to build personal connections?

Step 9: Provide students with the link to a career-search website in your state, if one is available. Give students a chance to explore the site during class, if possible.

Common Core Connection

- Determine meanings of domain-specific words in context
  CCSS.ELA-LITERACY.RST.11-12.4
- Integrate multiple sources of information from a variety of media
  CCSS.ELA-LITERACY.RST.11-12.7
- Use precise language and domain-specific vocabulary
  CCSS.ELA-LITERACY.WHST.11-12.2D
- Conduct a short research project
  CCSS.ELA-LITERACY.WHST.11-12.7

WebQuest Your Career Path – Sample Research Card

(Blank printable card available by scanning the QR code on the previous page)

Career Planning: Inspector — RESEARCH CARD

Job Availability Between now – 2024: Will I be entering a field that is projected to have plenty of opportunity to find work?
Yes

State & Area Data: Will I need to look beyond Indiana or is there a high demand in this region too? What would be another state to look for jobs with this career path?
High Demand in Indiana

Expected pay (Median pay): Will this job provide you with your expected lifestyle or is it a "stepping stone" to advance to another position within this industry?
No it doesn't pay enough

What are duties of this job that appeal to you?
Inspecting, easy

What do you like about the work environment data?
Not Stationary

Examine the Education Requirement And "How to Become One" section. Watch the video on the Career Onestop website. Does anything in the video make this career a good fit for you?
What are potential obstacles that could be difficult for you?
Easy to get into

Doesn't pay enough!

Incidental and Assessment Vocabulary

When you are choosing complex text (including video and multimedia materials) for your students, look out for words you can point out beyond the technical or academic terms. Find adult-like, academic words that students may have heard but do not use themselves, and encourage students to add them to their vocabulary word lists. A person's *incidental vocabulary* consists of words learned without having tried to learn them. We are much more likely to pick up on these words if they are explicitly taught and repeated. Many incidental vocabulary terms are commonly used in assessment questions. Knowing an academic word (or a word's second meaning in a new context) can mean the difference between understanding and misunderstanding an author or a test question. We refer to incidental vocabulary words that are commonly used on tests as *assessment vocabulary*. For example, a student might be proficient in the actual content knowledge, but if a question asks if a statement "underscores" a certain idea, the student who misunderstands "underscore" may not be able to answer the question. This type of vocabulary is especially important if you have any students for whom English is not their first language (EL learners). All students will be more prepared for understanding text—also for understanding test questions—if you build up their incidental and assessment vocabulary.

Examples of incidental and assessment vocabulary:

Article	"What is the main idea of the *article*?"
Best	"Which statement *BEST* identifies the author's purpose?"
Capitalize	"Industry leaders must *capitalize* on their strengths."
Contain	"Which sentences *contain* indirect references?"
Contribute	"How did new technology *contribute* to industry growth?"
Describe	"*Describe* the properties of this machinery."
Detail	"Support your answer with *details* from the text."
Explain	"Which sentence *explains* the author's reasoning?"
Incident	"The *incident* resulted from several previous accidents."
Influence	"How did this event *influence* the larger economy?"
Meaning	"What is the author's intended *meaning* of the word 'properties'?"
Most likely	"Choose the outcome that is *MOST LIKELY*."
Properties	"Describe the *properties* of this machinery."
Select	"He *selected* the most prestigious of the *select* schools listed."
Statement	"Which *statement* best describes the process?"
Support	"*Support* your answer with evidence from the text."
Underscore	"The author's use of simple terms *underscores* her main point."

Making It Work – Deepening Understanding of Vocabulary with SWRL

- How can I combine the lab and the classroom to deepen my students' understanding of vocabulary terms?

- How can I encourage speaking, writing, reading, and listening to include regular use of vocabulary terms?

Notes:

PART 2: PRODUCTIVE TALK

IN THIS SECTION

What is Productive Talk?
Physical Tools for Productive Talk
Seven Norms for Discussion
Carousel
Post-It Note Tug-of-War
Gather the Facts
Paired Reading
Question Fishbowl
Affinity Diagram (Brainstorming in Categories)
Flow Chart (Brainstorming Processes)
Concept Map (Brainstorming Attributes and Features)
Decision Tree (Brainstorming to Analyze)
Five Whys (Brainstorming the Roots of a Problem)
Cause-Effect Brainstorming
SWOT Analysis (Brainstorming through Different Lenses)
Choices and Consequences (Brainstorming Possibilities)
Teacher Activity: Feedback Prediction Guide

What Is Productive Talk?

In Part 1 on vocabulary, we emphasized that your vocabulary program should include daily Speaking, Writing, Reading, and Listening (SWRL). In this section, we want to emphasize the power of speaking and listening between students—in short, what is known as productive talk. Productive talk is, quite simply, speaking that leads to learning. It happens during conversations in which students do most of the talking, while teachers guide them to listen to each other, explain their thinking, question and challenge each other's ideas, and revise their own opinions based on input from others. Brainstorming, small-group discussions, peer Q&A sessions, and public presentations can all be productive talk.

Why Productive Talk Improves Literacy (The Scientific Answer)

Brain research shows that the strength of the *arcuate fasciculus*—a bundle of axons that connects the brain's two speech centers—directly affects our ability to learn words; and that articulating new words strengthens the arcuate fasciculus (López-Barroso et. al., 2013). Student conversation, therefore, is not simply a nice break from lecturing or a check for understanding. Conversation is a key to improving literacy.

When people participate actively in conversation, their brains sync up, mirroring and anticipating the neural activity of the others in the conversation (Stephens, Silbert and Hasson, 2010). Engaging in conversation as we learn, rather than simply listening to new information, helps make this neural activity more likely. As we learn, our brains forge and strengthen new pathways through which information can travel. The human brain contains close to 100 billion brain cells, called neurons, and they are all networked together. Neurons transmit electrical signals that travel through these pathways, creating meaning and delivering information. But blocking each connection is a tiny gap, called a synapse. When we learn something new, the electrical signal has to jump across the gap, forging a new path. The first time we encounter new information, it can be difficult for our brains to bridge that gap. Like blazing a new trail, connecting neurons isn't always straightforward, and it takes great effort. But frequent use strengthens the new pathway, and makes future journeys there easier. Learning is

> **Reading Tip: Prediction encourages productive talk!**
>
> Why do we read? For entertainment and for information! If you doubt a text will engage students through pleasure, then you need to design your reading activity around another purpose: to find specific information that will lead to productive talk.
>
> Tap into the magic of prediction to enhance the productive talk activities in this section. Throughout any activity, ask questions about what students think will happen, and use their answers to get them talking afterwards. In addition to the activities in this section, use the prediction guide on page 168 with any prepared reading or lab activity to structure great conversations.

about creating and strengthening these neural pathways, which happens readily in conversation with others (BBC Worldwide, 1998).

Productive talk allows students to examine information from a variety of perspectives, reinforcing their neural connections by requiring that they use them repeatedly in both speaking and listening. This reinforcement is called overlearning, and it causes those neural pathways to widen and deepen. Like a cable with many strands, an understanding that includes multiple experiences and viewpoints adds strength and dimension, establishing the new information in the brain so that it can then lead to even more new understandings (Beach, 2013). Productive talk provides a tool for overlearning that keeps students' brains actively engaged.

Why Productive Talk Improves Literacy (The Practical Answer)

Productive talk allows you to teach responsively, using students' questions, comments, and disagreements as entry points into the materials and standards, guiding students to the curriculum instead of delivering the curriculum to the students. The critical reading, analyzing, and arguing with evidence that are emphasized by the Common Core Literacy Standards can all be practiced during productive talk about your own content area. Students understand and retain more when they have explained information in their own words. Productive talk also uses their collective background knowledge to put new information into context, constructing meaning socially. Education researcher John Hattie has demonstrated that the teaching strategies with the largest effect involve approaches in which student talk is fundamental (Hattie, 2009). Productive talk is a chance for both high- and low-level readers to shine, building self-efficacy while practicing their literacy skills. Speaking, writing, reading, and listening are all intricately related skills. Speaking and listening allow students to solidify their learning, reflect on their prior knowledge, and prepare for critical reading and writing. (source learning pyramid?) When students shape the conversation, they stay interested, and they find a purpose for the reading.

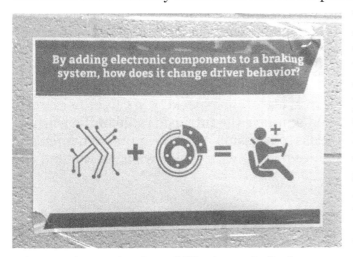

Automotive teacher Darrell Wattley periodically posts laminated "essential questions" on his classroom wall to spark curiosity and encourage discussion that goes beyond textbook answers.

Productive talk works well in CTE classrooms because it is not something that must be done sitting alone at a desk. And using it to improve literacy isn't just a way for you to help your ELA teachers out. Implementing better literacy learning strategies will make you a more effective teacher in your content area, and it will prepare your students for their future in the field. It prepares them to explain their thinking and have technical discussions aloud, skills valued highly by prospective employers, who may disregard a great resume if the candidate doesn't communicate well. Practicing communication skills way beyond reading will make students better learners and more successful mechanics, cosmetologists, law enforcement officers, and business owners of all kinds.

Essential Conditions for Productive Talk

To make the most of productive talk, you need an environment in which everyone feels welcome to participate. To that end, we have specifically included strategies that can be used to de-emphasize grades, eliminate "busy work," encourage metacognition, and tailor your instruction to multiple learning styles. These four elements are at the heart of student engagement, and they will help make your productive talk more effective in promoting literacy skills.

De-emphasize Grades

Productive talk will flourish when your classroom culture promotes learning for its own sake. Decades of research from as far back as 1933 have made it clear that grades are often problematic (Kohn, 2011). Reliance on grades reduces students' interest in the material, the quality of their thinking, and their intrinsic drive to take intellectual risks (Kohn, 2011). Risk-averse learners "downshift" their brains into a kind of survival mode, looking for the right answer instead of seeking understanding (Rutherford, p. 103, 2014). People do better creative work and engage more readily in learning when they know that what they're doing is relevant beyond a quantitative assessment. When we rely on external rewards to motivate others, we may unintentionally undermine their intrinsic motivation (Pink, 2009) and risk extinguishing their love of learning. Especially in career field work, it is important for students to internalize and embrace the intrinsic value of the learning that could become their life's work. A class discussion will be more dynamic and productive when students, freed from a preoccupation with their own achievement, can take interest in the topic itself.

There are better ways than quizzes and tests to assess progress, and better ways than quantitative grades to communicate that progress. The American education world has been slow to respond to the research on a policy level, but that doesn't mean you must give grades all the power in your own classroom. Even within a system that requires grades every nine weeks, you can de-emphasize their impact in your daily classroom work. Ungraded productive talk provides opportunities to do just that. It allows for more holistic informal assessments, so you can gradually reduce or eliminate your reliance on quizzes and tests. It gives students the dignity of tasks that are challenging, interesting, and meaningful. To get the most from the activities in this book, we suggest that you reduce your reliance on quantitative grades in your classroom. Productive talk activities work best when they are ungraded, or at least when grades are de-emphasized and are used to assess students qualitatively instead. Provide descriptive, actionable feedback comments on student work periodically, according to the progress they're making in their thought process, rather than focusing solely on the outcome. Some teachers find it helpful to create rubrics that include qualitative goals, such as student "agency," or how a student takes ownership and initiative in the learning. At the end of the semester or grading period, consider using two-way discussions with students and qualitative assessments to decide on a grade, if necessary. Some teachers even ask the students themselves, at the end of an ongoing conversation, what grade they think they earned. They almost always choose the same grade that the teacher would have chosen for them (Kohn, 2011). However you decide to go about it, work to gradually replace a reliance on grades with an emphasis on qualitative, meaningful assessments during productive talk activities.

You may meet some initial resistance from students who are addicted to grades, but they'll likely find that a qualitative approach actually expands their opportunities for excellence. Grades oversimplify, and de-emphasizing them makes room for a more complete understanding of student progress and a fuller picture of their achievements. It may take a bit more time and attention up front, but it will pay off in a classroom environment where students participate more readily in productive talk and ultimately learn more.

Eliminate "Busy Work"

Student-led work has tremendous potential for learning and for uncovering topics and ideas for discussion, but it requires more than simply avoiding the teacher-centered lecture model. Students should spend large amounts of class time speaking and learning from each other, and any independent work should be designed to help students reflect, explore more deeply, and contribute more to their collaborative work. There simply is not time for work that is not meaningful to students. Meaningful work allows students to think deeply, reorganize content in their brains, and make connections between ideas that will solidify the learning. Self-directed or not, if your students are spending their time on basic worksheets meant to check for understanding, the ensuing productive talk will be less effective. The literacy strategies in this book are intended to help you frame activities that allow students to construct meaning for themselves while giving you a more effective and efficient means of checking for understanding. It's not enough to cover the material. Productive talk allows students to absorb the material.

Encourage Metacognition

The word *metacognition* means thinking about thinking. When students think deeply and construct meaning for themselves, they will inevitably engage in multiple thought processes, which they need to be able to identify. An awareness of their own thought processes allows students to zoom out and see themselves and their classmates from a distance, where they can think critically and evaluate multiple perspectives. This distancing effect lets students revise and rearrange their ideas and see how things connect. Being able to explain their thinking allows for more meaningful, nuanced discussions, and it gives you, the teacher, a valuable window into their understanding. Far from being an "extra" layer that describes the learning, metacognition itself pushes students into more complex thinking.

To encourage metacognition, you should model it, explaining your thought process as you introduce information. Beyond modeling, you can teach your students to label their thinking and that of their classmates during discussion times, as well as using specific mind-mapping activities, such as a Concept Map (p.120). Metacognition takes practice, and it is not strongly correlated to IQ (Stanovich, 2009), so there's no need to reserve this kind of thinking for advanced classes or top students. Give all your students a common language that allows them to explain their understanding, and establish this language as a norm of productive talk in your classroom. If you use verbs such as *classify*, *analyze*, *predict*, and *synthesize* to identify what students are doing during discussions, be sure to have students explain these processes as they identify them. You want students to be able to say, "I disagree with you because I'm looking at the problem this way, and you seem to be looking at it that way."

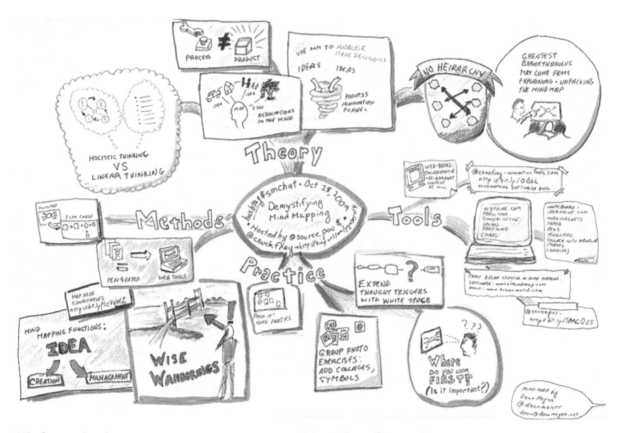

Mind mapping is one way to encourage metacognition. Photo © 2010 by Dean Meyers, licensed via creative commons. Scan this QR code to view on Flickr.

Physical Tools for Productive Talk

You may find the following props helpful during some productive talk activities:

1. **Dry erase boards** - After one student answers a question aloud, the class usually moves on, even if other students had not yet finished thinking through the question. Rather than calling on one student to speak, give every student the chance to complete the thought process by writing their answers on individual dry erase boards. Expecting a response from every student means they will all be more prepared to speak.

2. **Popsicle sticks/ Deck of name cards** - To keep every student engaged during discussions, keep a jar of popsicle sticks with all your students' names on them, or a deck of name cards you can put in your pocket. Randomly draw a name each time you need to call on a student, and then put the name back in the jar, where it will be possible to draw it again. You may not always be able to hear from every student, but this method ensures that every student always has the possibility of being called upon, encouraging them to be prepared for participation.

3. **Clipboards** - Encourage literacy skills in the lab by giving each student a clipboard. This allows them to record vocabulary words, annotate diagrams, and record questions during demonstrations, while interacting with real physical objects. Students are more prepared for productive talk in the classroom when they can more easily make connections to lab experiences.

4. **Notecards** – Make note-taking more versatile with notecards. When students write key ideas on notecards instead of in notebooks, they can use their notes more often. They can re-structure their notes, use certain topics for discussion, and categorize words and ideas. Notecards allow students to isolate key ideas so they can go back over certain topics for review.

5. **Post-it Notes** – Build students' confidence in participation by using Post-it notes. For students who hesitate to share their ideas, these sticky notes allow them to jot down ideas they could share later. They also allow groups of students to stick their

ideas to a wall and move them around, reorganizing them. Post-it notes provide a little bit of anonymity while still creating accountability.

6. **Chart Paper** – Create interactive versions of the graphic organizers in this book by having students draw them on large sheets of paper taped to walls around the classroom. Many students—especially in CTE—learn best in a lab setting, when they can get out of their seats, move around, and interact with others. Chart paper can help you make the classroom as much like the lab as possible.

7. **Norms for Discussion** – Post a large, visible list of collaborative norms, and remind your students of them whenever you begin discussion. If you've ever dreaded a staff meeting or class discussion because you know someone will dominate the conversation, you understand the need for group norms. Collaborators must adhere to an explicit, agreed-upon set of rules to make the conversation flow smoothly and productively. Especially in CTE, students need to learn how to discuss professional topics without dominating and without having to be invited in. The suggested norms on the following page assist in diplomacy, according to the U.S. Department of State.

Chart paper and Post-it notes combine to increase productive talk opportunities.

Seven Norms for Discussion

1. **Pausing** – Slowing down the back-and-forth of conversation gives listeners "wait time" for improved critical thinking and better decision making. It promotes more purposeful responses and it tells others that their comments are worth thinking about. Students may be uncomfortable with silence at first, so emphasize the importance of pausing.

2. **Paraphrasing** – Translating someone else's idea into your own words helps others see your thought process, understand the idea better, and evaluate information more accurately. Paraphrasing a classmate's contribution to the discussion is also a respectful way to show you want to understand their statement.

3. **Probing** – Asking clarifying questions to understand an idea helps the whole group to think more precisely, and it shows others that their ideas are worth the effort to understand.

4. **Putting forward ideas** – Sharing original and personal contributions is vital to collaboration. Encourage everyone to share ideas, and make an effort to build up self-confidence and a sense of security so that ideas will be put forward.

5. **Paying attention to self and others** – Understanding how others process ideas leads to better partnerships. Students should make themselves aware of differences between their and others' communication styles, personal backgrounds, and ways of thinking, so that they will be able to accept disagreements.

6. **Presuming positive presuppositions** – For group work to be productive, it is necessary to assume the other group members have good intentions, even when they disagree. Presuming positive presuppositions allows members to "play devil's advocate" or to debate an idea without personal enmity. Impress upon students the importance of communicating positive assumptions about others.

7. **Pursuing a balance between advocacy and inquiry** – Advocating for a position must be balanced with inquiring about the positions of others. Good collaborators do both, demonstrating a desire to learn as part of the group, and promoting equity in discussions.

(Overseas Schools Advisory Council, 2004)

The Carousel

"I wish every student would participate in discussions!"

The Why

As quick as: 20 minutes

Multiple learning styles:

The Carousel promotes equity, because more students are likely to speak productively when groups are small and critiques or disagreements are indirect.

Gist: an extended, active version of Think-Pair-Share. The carousel gets everyone moving around the room to write and discuss various topics.

When to use: As a pre-assessment or a review game of a broad, multifaceted topic. When you need to involve everyone instead of hearing from the same few students each time.

How It Works

Step 1: Post 4-5 large sheets of paper around the room, with plenty of space between them. On each paper, write a different question or statement that can elicit a broad range of responses.

Step 2: Divide your students into 4-5 teams, and give each team a different colored marker. Each group begins at a different one of the posted questions.

Step 3: Set a timer for two minutes (or other amount of time). Instruct students as follows: "When I say go, you will have two minutes as a group to write as many intelligent points as you can on your board. When I call time, every group will take their marker and rotate to the left, just like a carousel."

Step 4: When groups rotate, instruct students as follows: "Before you write anything on your new question, read through what the other group(s) wrote. If you disagree with something they have written, put one line through that statement and write a response to it. Then begin to post your own additional thoughts."

Step 5: Continue rotating until all groups have responded to every question. Then facilitate a class discussion. All it takes to get great conversation going is a couple of lines drawn through comments of another color.

Twist: To cover a topic on which your students have background knowledge, try carousel to condense classroom study time. Pull out headings from the text to create your open-ended questions, ensuring that all necessary aspects of the topic will be covered during discussion.

Part 2: Productive Talk

Student perspective: "I'm more comfortable sharing my ideas in short, written statements first with my small group before the whole-class discussion. And it's fun!"

Common Core Connection

- Cite textual evidence
  CCSS.ELA-LITERACY.RST.11-12.1
- Summarize complex concepts by paraphrasing
  CCSS.ELA-LITERACY.RST.11-12.2
- Determine meanings of domain-specific words in context
  CCSS.ELA-LITERACY.RST.11-12.4
- Synthesize information from various sources into a coherent understanding
  CCSS.ELA-LITERACY.RST.11-12.9
- Work toward proficient independent understanding of text
  CCSS.ELA-LITERACY.RST.11-12.10
- Use precise language and domain-specific vocabulary
  CCSS.ELA-LITERACY.WHST.11-12.2D

ASKING THE RIGHT QUESTIONS

To generate thoughtful discussion during the Carousel, or any other time, ask open-ended questions that encourage students to think about context, not questions that have simple correct answers. For example, in an agriculture class, instead of asking which tools are used by horticulturists, ask how a horticulturist might handle a specific plant species in a specific environment.

Here are a few ways to generate thought-provoking, open-ended questions:

1. Use question stems from page 108. You may even combine a few related questions in one prompt.

2. Ask "essential questions." Essential questions are those "big idea" questions that make your field relevant and drive professionals. For our agriculture example, an essential question might be, "How is horticulture beneficial or damaging to the environment?"

3. Give context to "essential questions." Use current events, local situations, or your students' personal experiences to make essential questions more specific. For example, the essential question above could become, "How might genetic engineering of affect our local economy?"

4. Pose problems to be solved. Present a hypothetical situation as your Carousel prompt. "You've discovered an overabundance of nitrogen in a stream near your property. Is this a good or bad thing? What are some possible causes, and what should you do next?"

Post-It Note Tug-of-War

"My students need help tapping into their prior knowledge!"

Gist: A more physically engaging way to brainstorm. Students in two groups race to post as many details as possible about their topic.

When to use: To review prior knowledge by comparing and contrasting two ideas, people, products, theories, or data sets. Use this activity to prepare students to write, solve a problem hands-on, or make a decision by evaluating two opposing arguments or choices.

The Why

As quick as: 3 minutes

Multiple learning styles:

Tapping into the affective domain with an active game reminds students that classroom learning is fun, just like the lab.

How It Works

Step 1 Choose 2 topics and write them on the board on opposite sides of the room. If possible, include a photo or other visual representation. Depending on your subject, this could be two types of the same product, two mechanical parts of a machine, two influential people, or any other two topics related to your study.

Step 2 Divide the class into 2 groups, and give four or five Post-it notes to each student. Assign one group to each of the topics you have posted.

Step 3 Set a timer. Challenge student groups to write a descriptive detail or other relevant information on each Post-it note and race to post their details on the wall under their topic. They should write concepts and ideas that can later be used for discussion or writing, rather than one-word responses. The side with the most Post-it notes wins.

Step 4 As the teacher, you will be the "knot" in the tug-of-war rope, moving to the side of the wall with the most Post-its during the brainstorm session.

Step 5 Afterwards, sort the Post-it notes as a class, comparing and contrasting each detail with corresponding details from the other topic. If desired, expand the activity, challenging students to write from a prompt, using details from the Post-it notes.

Twist: Divide students into more than 2 groups, and for each topic use a part of the same machine or product. For example, each group brainstorms about an ingredient in the same dish (culinary), or a part of an engine (auto). Afterwards, challenge students to explain how the parts work together in the whole.

Student perspective: "Comparing and contrasting helps me think more deeply, and doing it as a physical activity wakes me up and gets me involved."

Common Core Connection

- Cite textual evidence
  CCSS.ELA-LITERACY.RST.11-12.1
- Summarize complex concepts by paraphrasing
  CCSS.ELA-LITERACY.RST.11-12.2
- Determine meanings of domain-specific words in context
  CCSS.ELA-LITERACY.RST.11-12.4
- Analyze how text structures information into categories
  CCSS.ELA-LITERACY.RST.11-12.5
- Integrate and evaluate multiple diverse sources to solve a problem
  CCSS.ELA-LITERACY.RST.11-12.7
- Evaluate hypotheses, data, analyses, and conclusions; Corroborate or challenge conclusions with additional information
  CCSS.ELA-LITERACY.RST.11-12.8
- Synthesize information from various sources into a coherent understanding
  CCSS.ELA-LITERACY.RST.11-12.9
- Work toward proficient independent understanding of text
  CCSS.ELA-LITERACY.RST.11-12.10
- Use precise language and domain-specific vocabulary
  CCSS.ELA-LITERACY.WHST.11-12.2D

Post-its make brainstorming active and give students the freedom to rearrange their thoughts. Add accountability by giving each group a different color. The easily visible notes encourage students to share original thoughts.

Gather the Facts

"My students think informational reading is boring!"

Gist: Students must read with the purpose of remembering facts and then report those facts as a whole class without looking back at the text.

When to Use: When reading technical materials, manuals, and other text that lacks opportunities for readers to make a personal connection. Increase engagement by giving an explicit purpose for reading something they otherwise wouldn't find exciting, while avoiding the "look-and-find" method.

The Why

As quick as: 15 minutes

Multiple learning styles:

How It Works

Step 1: Choose a text (about a 3-page selection) and read it yourself ahead of time. Time yourself reading it, and add a couple minutes; this will help you plan enough time for reading in class.

Step 2: Say to students, "This section of the text contains a lot of important facts. To help make the facts 'stick,' we are going to use a memory challenge game. You will read silently, and you may annotate or take notes. But once the reading time is over, you will not be able to look at the text or your notes. Then, I will ask each of you to tell me 3 specific facts from the text. Our goal as a class is to end up with a complete and diverse list of facts, with everyone contributing some new information."

Step 3: Remind students that this activity is a cooperative challenge. The whole class will succeed or struggle together, and the final product can be turned into a useful study guide. Those who share their facts toward the end will have a hard time coming up with new information, but reassure them that you'll switch up the order for the next round.

Step 4: Time the silent reading, and then instruct students to put away their texts and notes.

Step 5: Call on students to report their facts, and write them on the board or type onto a projector screen as you go (or have students get up and add them to a large graphic organizer on the board). Even if the students' "facts" are not 100% correct, write them and allow students the opportunity to correct them or add to them.

Step 6: Once everyone's facts have been written (and corrected, as needed), you can begin the activity again with another section of text. I find this activity successful for up to 3 rounds. Beyond that, students begin to lose steam.

Step 7: Have students record your fact list themselves, or print it off for them to keep as a study guide.

Twist: Take it a step further. Once your board is covered with facts, pair students up and have them create a graphic organizer that shows the relationship between the facts (categorizing them, showing cause/effect, etc.). Most partners end up creating different types of organizers, which can lead to great class discussion and productive talk. You can also challenge students to organize and categorize the facts into a coherent outline of the text to save as a study guide.

Student Perspective: "I like the challenge of remembering tidbits from what I read, and it's nice that it becomes our study guide. When I'm using it to study later, I can remember things more easily because I remember making it."

Common Core Connection

- Cite textual evidence
  CCSS.ELA-LITERACY.RST.11-12.1
- Summarize complex concepts by paraphrasing
  CCSS.ELA-LITERACY.RST.11-12.2
- Determine meanings of domain-specific words in context
  CCSS.ELA-LITERACY.RST.11-12.4
- Analyze how text structures information into categories
  CCSS.ELA-LITERACY.RST.11-12.5
- Work toward proficient independent understanding of text
  CCSS.ELA-LITERACY.RST.11-12.10
- Use precise language and domain-specific vocabulary
  CCSS.ELA-LITERACY.WHST.11-12.2D

Paired Reading (Paired Listening/Paired Demonstration)

"My students don't take ownership of difficult information. It's in one ear, out the other!"

Gist: Student pairs take turns reading passages of text (or listening, or demonstrating in the lab) paraphrasing it to each other as they go.

When to Use: During any reading (watching, listening) activity, when you want to be sure they are actively engaging the text instead of getting lost in the details. You can use paired reading even if you did not prepare for it ahead of time. This strategy is so effective because it is so simple! Great for health careers classes.

The Why

As quick as: 5 minutes

Multiple learning styles:

How It Works

Step 1: Group students into pairs. One begins as the "teller" and one as the "listener." They will alternate in these roles. Student pairs should share one textbook (if you are using this strategy during a participatory demonstration, they should share one physical object). This activity would also be good in a lab, using clipboards, to close the gap between classroom and lab. Each student should also have a notebook and pencil.

Step 2: Both teller and listener quietly read a selection of text that is 1-3 paragraphs in length. Then they close the book (or pause the demonstration and put down the object) because it is important that what comes next be the students' own words.

Step 3: The "teller" then paraphrases the passage in his or her own words. Encourage "tellers" to bring up any personal experiences that the passage brings to mind, or any similar concepts that they are reminded of.

Step 4: The "listener" then responds, giving feedback about the teller's interpretation. Encourage listeners to ask questions, and to voice any points of disagreement about the meaning of the text. (It is a good idea to establish classroom norms for how to give useful feedback. See page 97 for a list of suggested norms.)

Step 5: After "teller" and "listener" have come to an agreement that the paraphrase was accurate, they should write a quick summary in their notebooks. Bullet points are helpful for summarizing the main points. (Be sure to explain the difference between paraphrasing and summarizing: paraphrasing is restating the text in your own words; summarizing is distilling it down to main points. Both skills are used in this activity.)

Step 6: Teachers should walk among the students throughout this activity, listening to how students paraphrase as a check for their understanding, and prompting them if necessary. It is not important that the teacher hear every word from every student; it is more important that every student get a chance to put the text in his or her own words.

Step 7: Switch roles: "Teller" and "listener" switch and repeat the process for the next couple of paragraphs.

Twist: Adapt this method when students are witnessing a demonstration or working in the lab, instead of reading. Pause throughout the demonstration, allowing partners to paraphrase what they have seen (or what their partner has demonstrated, if it is a participatory demonstration), and then summarize the main points being demonstrated, taking turns as above.

Twist 2: Use paired reading with a T-chart for students to determine similarities and differences between the information in the reading and a concept they already know. Have students draw a vertical line down the middle of a paper, and a horizontal line across the top, labeling "similarities to [original concept]" and "differences from [original concept]." Students should take turns paraphrasing the information by telling how it is similar or different from the previously-learned information, and providing feedback/asking questions. At the end, pairs should write a short summary that compares and contrasts the two concepts. By comparing and contrasting the reading with prior knowledge, students synthesize new information into their existing understanding.

Student Perspective: "I feel respected when I'm given the chance to help teach or explain something in my own words."

Common Core Connection

- Summarize complex concepts by paraphrasing
  CCSS.ELA-LITERACY.RST.11-12.2
- Determine meanings of domain-specific words in context
  CCSS.ELA-LITERACY.RST.11-12.4
- Analyze how text structures information into categories
  CCSS.ELA-LITERACY.RST.11-12.5
- Work toward proficient independent understanding of text
  CCSS.ELA-LITERACY.RST.11-12.10
- Use precise language and domain-specific vocabulary
  CCSS.ELA-LITERACY.WHST.11-12.2D

Question Fishbowl

"My students don't ask very compelling questions during discussion. They need prompting!"

Gist: Students choose random question stems, generate thoughtful questions, and rotate through a circle, speed-dating style, to stimulate discussion.

When to use: When student discussions don't take off on their own; to help students learn to generate thoughtful questions and practice productive talk in a low-pressure environment. See "Why Question Stems" on page 109 for further explanation.

The Why

As quick as: 20 minutes

Multiple learning styles:

To see a variation of collaborative questioning on video, scan the QR code below.

How It Works

Step 1 (before class): Print a list of numerous question stems (see list on the next page), cut them out individually, fold them in half, and put them inside a fishbowl or hat. Place the bowl on a desk or table during class.

Step 2: Write a topic or theme on the board, or ask a student to identify the topic or theme of a text or film clip you have just completed.

Step 3: Instruct each student to draw one question stem from the bowl and use it to generate a few thoughtful questions related to the theme. Say, "You have 3 minutes to come up with your questions, all related to the theme on the board, and all somehow drawing from the question stem you picked." Not all question stems fit perfectly with every topic, so allow your students to interpret the stems loosely. The point is for them to follow a basic pattern and ask a thoughtful question.

Step 4: Have students stand in an inner and outer circle, facing each other like they would in speed dating.

Step 5: Conduct a "3-minute face-off," with each pair of facing students asking their questions and responding to them before a timer signals that it is time for the inner signal to rotate to the next person.

Step 6: Repeat as time allows. Save the question stems for future use. You can pull out a few of them during any discussion, without the "speed-dating" element.

Part 2: Productive Talk

Student perspective: "I feel less pressure when every pair is talking at the same time. And the question stems make it easier to get started."

Common Core Connection

- Cite textual evidence
  CCSS.ELA-LITERACY.RST.11-12.1
- Summarize complex concepts by paraphrasing
  CCSS.ELA-LITERACY.RST.11-12.2
- Analyze how text structures information into categories
  CCSS.ELA-LITERACY.RST.11-12.5
- Analyze author's purpose and identify unresolved issues
  CCSS.ELA-LITERACY.RST.11-12.6
- Integrate and evaluate multiple diverse sources to solve a problem
  CCSS.ELA-LITERACY.RST.11-12.7
- Synthesize information from various sources into a coherent understanding
  CCSS.ELA-LITERACY.RST.11-12.9
- Work toward proficient independent understanding of text
  CCSS.ELA-LITERACY.RST.11-12.10
- Use precise language and domain-specific vocabulary
  CCSS.ELA-LITERACY.WHST.11-12.2D

Question Stems

1. Can you show/tell me another way to _____?
2. If you knew _____, what would you say or do differently?
3. How is _____ similar to/different from _____?
4. What are the most important characteristics of _____?
5. In what other way might we show/illustrate _____?
6. What is the big idea/key concept that connects _____ & _____?
7. How does _____ relate to _____?
8. What ideas/details can you add to _____?
9. What is wrong with _____?
10. How can you "punch a hole" in the logic of _____?
11. What might you do differently if you conducted/designed _____?
12. What conclusions might be drawn from _____?
13. What question was _____ trying to answer? What problem was _____ trying to solve?
14. What do people assume about_____?
15. What might happen differently if _____?
16. What criteria might you use to judge/evaluate _____?
17. What evidence supports _____?
18. How can we prove _____?
19. How could we disprove _____?
20. How might this be viewed from the perspective of _____?
21. How would someone 20 years older/younger view _____?
22. How would someone from _____ culture see _____ differently?
23. What alternatives to _____ should be considered?
24. What approach strategy could you use to _____?
25. How else could you say _____?
26. What makes _____ popular/unpopular/important/unimportant?
27. What does _____ remind you of?
28. Who do you know who thinks the same way as _____ (author/person/group)?
29. If you could be any of the people we've studied, whom would you choose to be and why?

30. Were there any parts of this work that were confusing to you? What made them so?

31. If you could have discovered something from the text/video/lesson, which one would you want ownership of and why?

32. What do you feel is the most important word, phrase, or passage in this reading? Why?

33. How has _____ evolved over time?

34. What are some positive and negative aspects of _____?

Why Question Stems?

We asked a group of cosmetology students to generate their own questions, and here are a few that they came up with:
1. What are the five layers of the epidermis?
2. How many types of nail shapes are there? Name them.
3. What did the early Egyptians use to create makeup for their eyes, lips, and skin?
4. True or False: Never apply nail enhancement product over wet nail primer.
5. What does OSHA stand for?

These are very useful questions for a cosmetologist to be able to answer, but they do not push people into complex thought, so they make for stilted discussions. Use question stems to get students discussing these same topics, and they'll learn the facts while also practicing deeper thought and taking ownership of the information.

Here's the rewrite, using question stems from the list on the previous page:
1. What are some differences between the five layers of a toddler's epidermis and the layers of an 80-year-old's epidermis?
2. What makes various nail shapes more popular than others? Give examples.
3. How did early Egyptian makeup practices evolve, and can we see their impact on our culture today?
4. What would happen if you applied nail enhancement product over wet nail product? Has this ever happened to you?
5. What are some positive and negative aspects of OSHA?

Affinity Diagram (Brainstorming in Categories)

"My students need more structure to get them brainstorming."

Gist: Students organize concepts into categories or themes

When to use: To review a unit, or to prepare students for a writing assignment, presentation, or video demonstration. Their completed diagram will help them make an outline and plan their project.

The Why

As quick as: 10 minutes

Multiple learning styles:

How It Works

Step 1: Allow students to work in groups of 3 or 4, using one of the diagram variations on the following pages. Encourage engagement by having students create their own version of the organizer on a larger scale on the wall, to get them out of their seats.

Step 2: Say, "As a group, come up with what you think are the main themes of this topic. How would you divide it up if you were teaching it? Write those categories in the large boxes." Walk among students, facilitating, asking questions, and noting where they struggle.

Step 4: Say, "Now, as a group, remember details from the text, your notes, or activities we did in the lab. Decide which category each item fits into, and write it in one of the smaller boxes next to that category."

Note: If students are preparing to write a paper or create a project individually, stress that this step is for thinking aloud and bouncing ideas off each other, but that their diagrams should not look identical. They do not have to include every detail, but just those they deem relevant to the categories they have chosen.

Step 5: Continue facilitating. Once students have at least one detail in every box, they have enough content for an essay or presentation. They are now ready to create an outline, using the categories as main topics and using the details as supporting points. Then they will only need to expand on each point as they write.

Step 6: If they are not preparing to write or present, use the completed organizer for a larger class discussion. Students should generate a large list of themes or categories and discuss where each supporting detail fits. Since everyone has completed a diagram, expect participation from all.

 *Scan here for a video discussion of the affinity diagram.*

Common Core Connection

- Cite textual evidence
  CCSS.ELA-LITERACY.RST.11-12.1
- Summarize complex concepts by paraphrasing
  CCSS.ELA-LITERACY.RST.11-12.2
- Determine meanings of domain-specific words in context
  CCSS.ELA-LITERACY.RST.11-12.4
- Analyze how text structures information into categories
  CCSS.ELA-LITERACY.RST.11-12.5
- Work toward proficient independent understanding of text
  CCSS.ELA-LITERACY.RST.11-12.10
- Use precise language and domain-specific vocabulary
  CCSS.ELA-LITERACY.WHST.11-12.2D

- What are some topics in my discipline that can be broken down into categories?

- How can my students use the classification of ideas as a first step to a project?

Notes:

But I'm Not a Reading Teacher!

Affinity Diagram

Purpose:
To group ideas into categories or themes.

Procedure:
Record the results of a brainstorm by placing an organizing theme or heading in the larger boxes. Write similar concepts or items to the side of each theme or heading.

Affinity Diagram 2

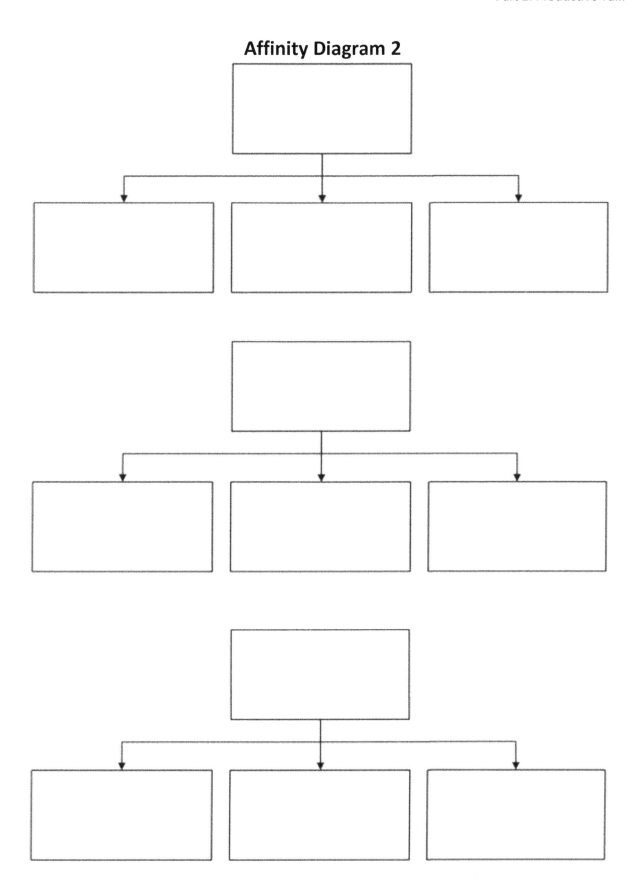

Flow Chart (Brainstorming Processes)

"Many students get frustrated because when they read, they just can't focus and remember what they have read."

The Why

As quick as: 3 minutes

Multiple learning styles:

Gist: Students pause during reading or lab work to collaboratively order the steps and restate the process.

When to use: During reading, when the text describes a process, to help chunk the text and develop active readers; or during lab work to help students construct meaning, and as a check for understanding.

How It Works

Step 1: Have students read a section of text or begin their lab work. Distribute one of the flow charts on the following pages.

Step 2: Say, "Now, let's make sense of the text (lab process). Close your books, pair up, and think through the steps you just read about. Discuss them together and begin to record them in the flow chart."

Step 3: Walk among students and check for correct understanding of the process.

Step 4: Have students continue reading or working in the lab. Continue pausing to complete the flow chart.

Step 5: Combine partnered groups into larger groups of 4 or 6 students, or come together as a class. Ask each pair to compare their processes and discuss possible problems that could occur if one step in the process malfunctions.

Twist: Instead of using individual flow charts, have small groups create their own charts on large sheets of paper to create instructional posters for the lab and get them out of their seats.

Twist 2: As a review or a check for understanding after reading or lab work, give students a list of words and phrases that are part of a process, and challenge them to order the steps correctly in the flow chart. Include fictitious steps so that students do not rely on a process of elimination. Then ask students to rank the steps by importance. In discussion, ask students to justify their rankings.

Common Core Connection

- Cite textual evidence
  CCSS.ELA-LITERACY.RST.11-12.1
- Summarize complex concepts by paraphrasing
  CCSS.ELA-LITERACY.RST.11-12.2
- Follow a complex multi-step procedure and analyze results based on explanations in the text
  CCSS.ELA-LITERACY.RST.11-12.3
- Determine meanings of domain-specific words in context
  CCSS.ELA-LITERACY.RST.11-12.4
- Synthesize information from various sources into a coherent understanding
  CCSS.ELA-LITERACY.RST.11-12.9
- Work toward proficient independent understanding of text
  CCSS.ELA-LITERACY.RST.11-12.10
- Use precise language and domain-specific vocabulary
  CCSS.ELA-LITERACY.WHST.11-12.2D

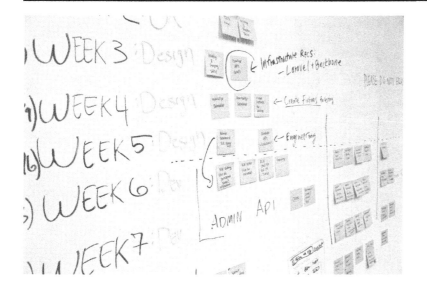

Consider creative ways to make flow charts, such as by using Post-it notes on the whiteboard, as shown.

Making It Work: Flow Charts

- What are some processes my students will learn about in my class?

- How can I incorporate visual representations of step-by-step processes into my existing lesson plans?

Notes:

Linear Flow Chart

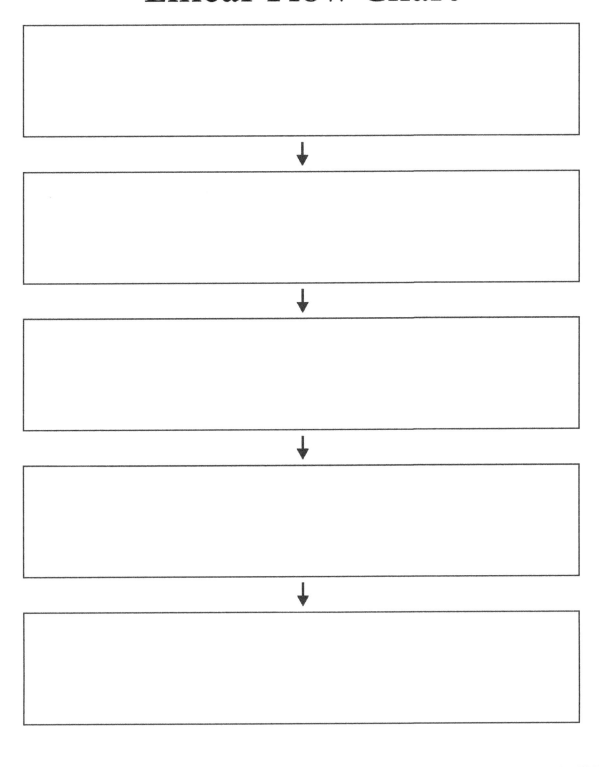

Cyclical Flow Chart

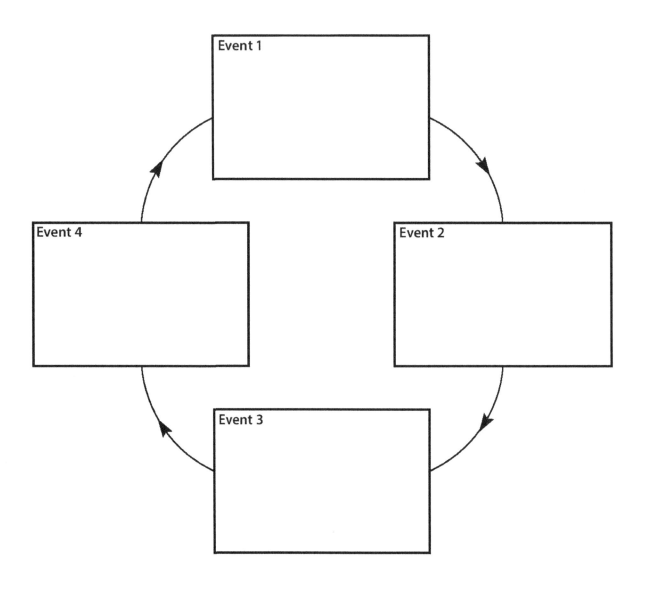

Part 2: Productive Talk

Cyclical Flow Chart

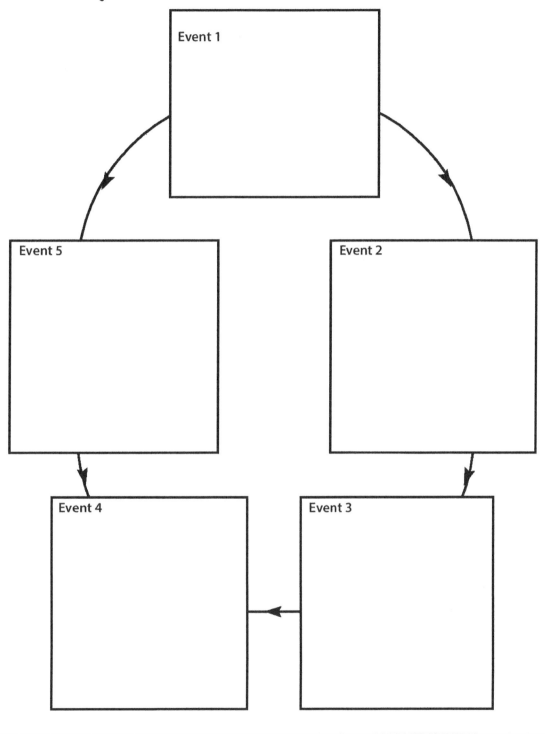

119

Concept Mapping (Brainstorming Attributes & Features)

"I need new ways to pre-assess my students' knowledge—not just another pre-quiz."

Gist: Students think about the details and attributes of several concepts within the same unit. Then students can collaborate over how the concepts relate to one another.

When to use: For pre-assessment before a new unit, or for post-assessment to analyze student understanding.

The Why

As quick as: 15 minutes

Multiple learning styles:

How It Works

Step 1: Divide students into groups of 3 or 4.

Step 2: Distribute to each group several blank copies of the graphic organizer on the following page, printed on half-size sheets of paper that can act as flash cards later.

Step 3: Distribute a list of terms and concepts. Remind students that each item on the list has attributes or examples that help define it.

Step 4: Say, "Designate one group member as the writer. You'll go through this list, writing each item in the center box on the concept map. As a group, try to identify at least 4 attributes or examples and write them in the outer boxes. I will set a timer for 30 seconds. When the timer goes off, you must move to the next concept, even if you haven't come up with 4 attributes."

Step 5: Set the timer to go off continually every 30 seconds, until groups have gone through each term or concept.

Step 6: Facilitate as your students work. If some groups seem to struggle, ask leading questions. If some groups are finishing before the timer, challenge them to include more details.

Step 7: After all terms have been covered, go through the list as a class, asking groups to share what they came up with, and allowing groups to fill in details they were missing. Each time someone shares, ask them to explain how the detail/attribute is related to the concept. If applicable, challenge students to identify the most important of the attributes listed, and why.

Twist: If using as a post-assessment tool, encourage students to explain the larger relationships between concepts on the list. Use large chart paper and have student groups draw an extended version of the concept map, connecting ideas together. Encourage critical thinking by presenting hypothetical situations or different contexts and asking which items from the list best apply.

> **Common Core Connection**
>
> - Cite textual evidence
>   CCSS.ELA-LITERACY.RST.11-12.1
> - Summarize complex concepts by paraphrasing
>   CCSS.ELA-LITERACY.RST.11-12.2
> - Determine meanings of domain-specific words in context
>   CCSS.ELA-LITERACY.RST.11-12.4
> - Analyze how text structures information into categories
>   CCSS.ELA-LITERACY.RST.11-12.5
> - Synthesize information from various sources into a coherent understanding
>   CCSS.ELA-LITERACY.RST.11-12.9
> - Work toward proficient independent understanding of text
>   CCSS.ELA-LITERACY.RST.11-12.10
> - Use precise language and domain-specific vocabulary
>   CCSS.ELA-LITERACY.WHST.11-12.2D

- Which concepts that I teach might be better understood if students used a concept map? What are some key terms that have several associated attributes, features, or results?

- What could students do with a concept map after creating it? How might they use it to teach, explain, present, or illustrate their work in a demonstration, in print, or online?

Notes:

A COMPLEX CONCEPT MAP

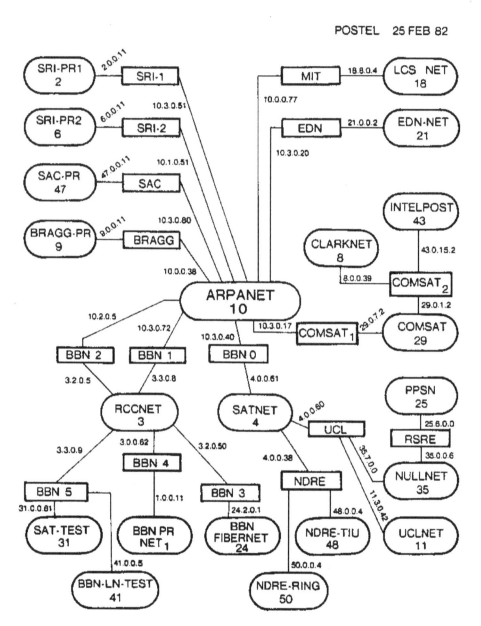

Concept maps can be simple, like the template on the following page, or they can be complex, like this map of the early Internet sourced from Wikipedia Commons. Whenever possible, encourage students to create their own concept maps on large paper instead of using the template. They'll have more freedom to expand and make more connections.

Part 2: Productive Talk

Concept Map

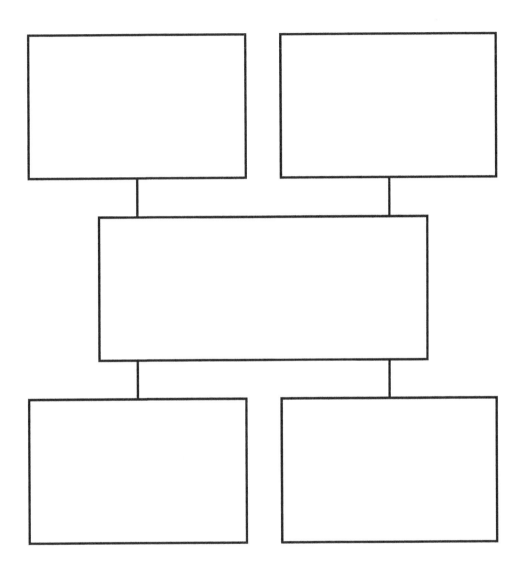

Purpose:
To define a concept by identifying its elements or attributes

Procedure:
Write the concepts in the center box. Record its attributes or elements in the out boxes

Decision Tree (Brainstorming to Analyze)

"My students tend to solve problems too quickly, without really thinking through different possible solutions."

Gist: The diagram helps slow down thought processes so students can analyze all aspects of a situation.

When to use: During problem solving in the lab, especially when teaching certification standards.

The Why

As quick as: 20 minutes

Multiple learning styles:

How It Works

Step 1 (before class): Plan a problem for students to solve. *Example: In early childhood education class, collect images of classroom environments that are incorrectly designed.*

Step 2: Group students in pairs or groups of 3-4. Give each group a decision tree diagram (p.126) BEFORE presenting the problem. This will prepare them with a visual representation of their task and get them thinking in terms of possible solutions as soon as they see the problem. We also recommend doing this activity in the lab instead of a classroom, and using clipboards. *Example: In our example above, students benefit from doing this activity in an early childhood classroom environment.*

Step 3: Explain the problem, and distribute corresponding images or props in the lab. *Example: Say, "This early childhood classroom would not pass inspection by a licensing bureau. Come up with the best possible solutions for bringing it up to standards."*

Step 4: Point groups to their notes, text, and ideas they have already learned. Example: *"Think in terms of ergonomics, state law, learning styles, privacy, affordability, safety, fun..."*

Twist: Have students physically solve the problem in the lab. *Example: Early childhood classroom has been incorrectly designed ahead of class. Students must go through the diagram and then physically correct the design of their own classroom.*

Student Perspective: "Without the diagram I would have solved the problem quickly without thinking through all the possibilities, and I wouldn't have found the best solution."

Common Core Connection

- Cite textual evidence
  CCSS.ELA-LITERACY.RST.11-12.1
- Summarize complex concepts by paraphrasing
  CCSS.ELA-LITERACY.RST.11-12.2
- Follow a complex multi-step procedure and analyze results based on explanations in the text
  CCSS.ELA-LITERACY.RST.11-12.3
- Integrate and evaluate multiple diverse sources to solve a problem
  CCSS.ELA-LITERACY.RST.11-12.7
- Evaluate hypotheses, data, analyses, and conclusions; Corroborate or challenge conclusions with additional information
  CCSS.ELA-LITERACY.RST.11-12.8
- Work toward proficient independent understanding of text
  CCSS.ELA-LITERACY.RST.11-12.10

Notes:

Possible problems/hypothetical situations I could set up for my students to solve:

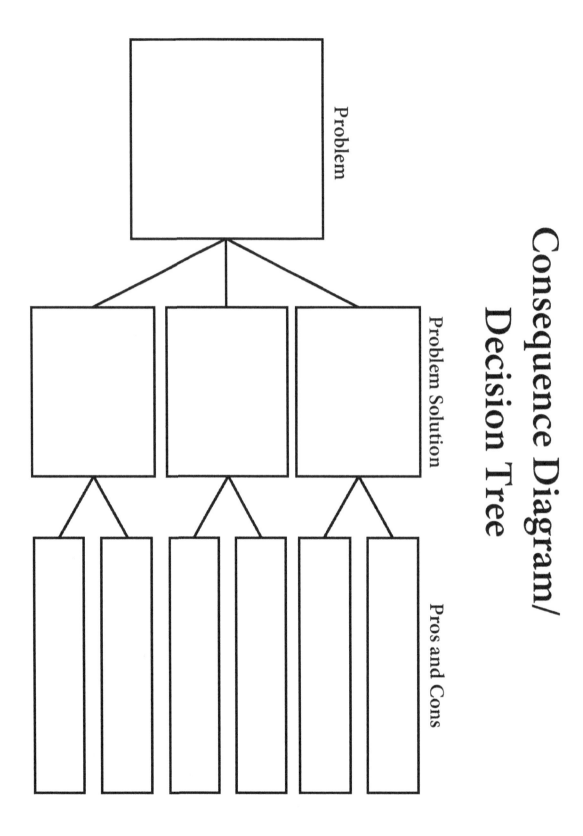

Part 2: Productive Talk

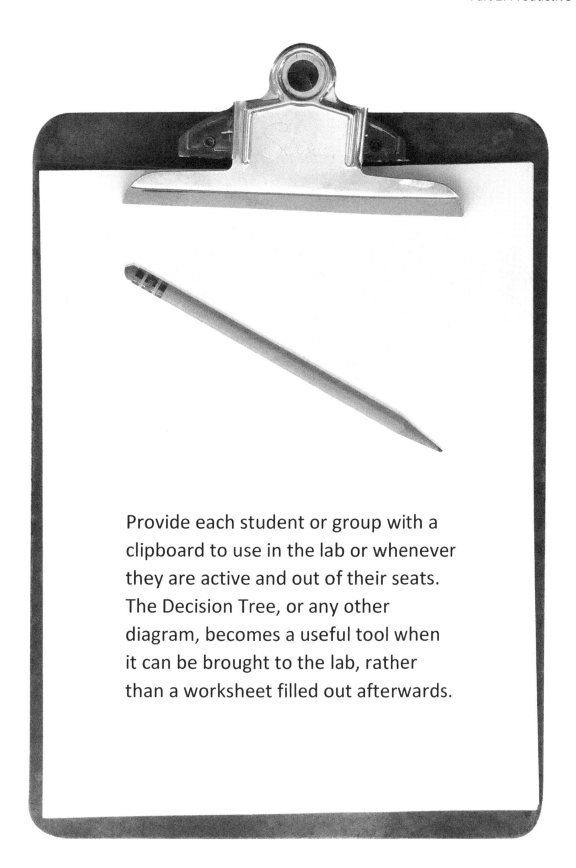

Provide each student or group with a clipboard to use in the lab or whenever they are active and out of their seats. The Decision Tree, or any other diagram, becomes a useful tool when it can be brought to the lab, rather than a worksheet filled out afterwards.

Five Whys (Brainstorming the Roots of a Problem)

Adapted from the I Six Sigma Five Whys Process (2016)

Gist: Students think backwards to identify the original roots of a problem (reverse of the decision tree on page 124).

When to use: While solving problems in the lab.

The Why

As quick as: 10 minutes

Multiple learning styles:

Just as the Decision Tree helps students think forward, the Five Whys helps them think backward, review, and connect the dots.

How It Works

Step 1: Have students work in groups or pairs.

Step 2: Distribute one of the graphic organizers on the following pages, or have student groups create their own as a large visual on the board with Post-it notes.

Step 3: Present students with a real or hypothetical problem. Challenge students to identify original sources of the problem.

Step 4: Instruct students to think aloud, starting with the problem and working backwards by speaking and writing the steps that may have led to the problem. Encourage discussion along the way.

Step 5: Bring student groups together to share the sources they identified. They may have identified multiple sources of the problem. Have them create a list and discuss how to avoid the problem in the future.

Twist: Take it further by having students write a paragraph or create a video explaining how the sources they identified can lead to problems, and how to avoid them. Find a way to make their writing or video useful in the future, such as including it in a long-term "How-To" manual project, or adding it to their own portfolio website.

Instead of treating the Five Whys as an extra visual aid for students, use it to structure a whole laboratory lesson, in which they move slowly through the steps to identify an actual problem with equipment or technology.

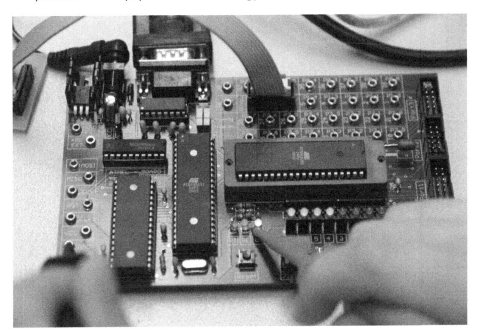

Common Core Connection

- Summarize complex concepts by paraphrasing
  CCSS.ELA-LITERACY.RST.11-12.2
- Analyze author's purpose and identify unresolved issues
  CCSS.ELA-LITERACY.RST.11-12.6
- Integrate and evaluate multiple diverse sources to solve a problem
  CCSS.ELA-LITERACY.RST.11-12.7
- Synthesize information from various sources into a coherent understanding
  CCSS.ELA-LITERACY.RST.11-12.9
- Work toward proficient independent understanding of text
  CCSS.ELA-LITERACY.RST.11-12.10
- Use precise language and domain-specific vocabulary
  CCSS.ELA-LITERACY.WHST.11-12.2D

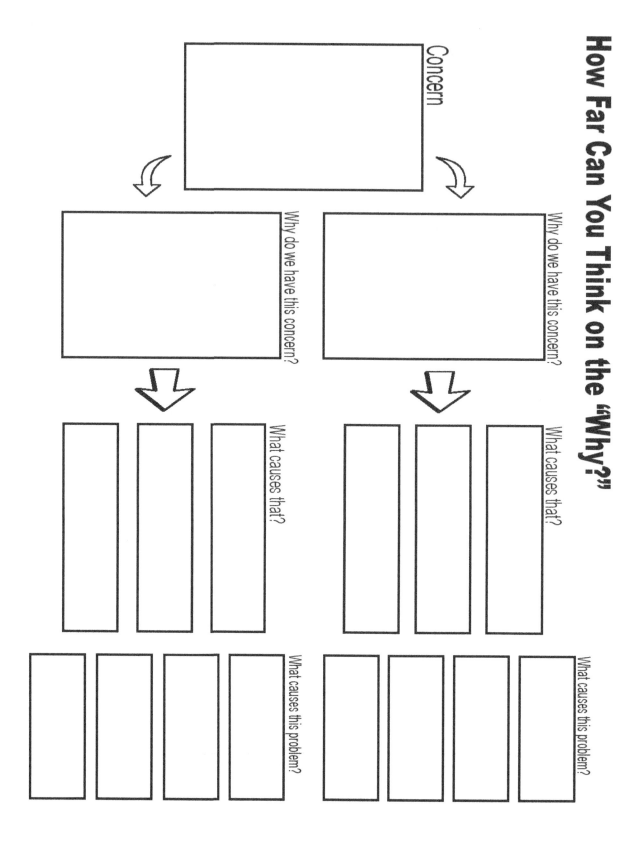

5 Why Analysis

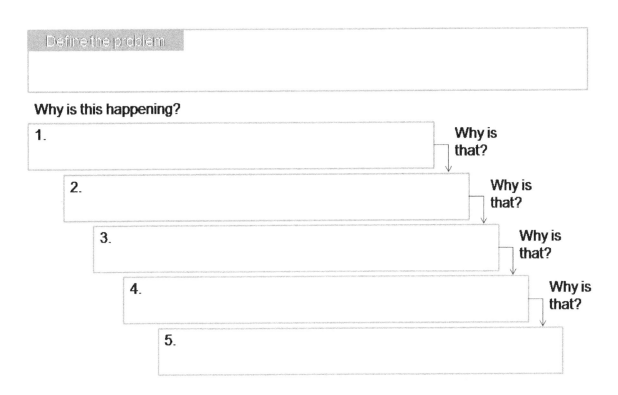

But I'm Not a Reading Teacher!

The 5 Whys: *Thinking deeply about a problem*

Our Problem:

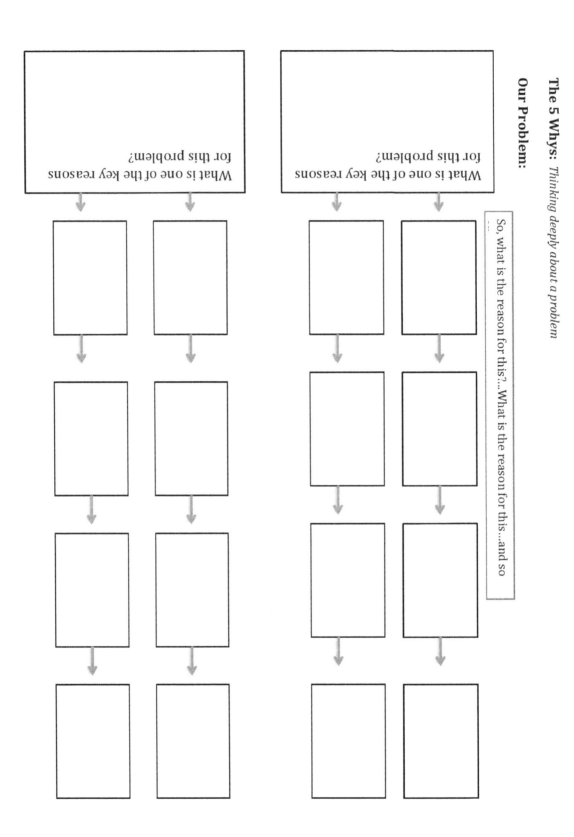

Making It Work – Five Whys

- What are some real-world problems my students can examine using diagrams such as the Five Whys organizer?

- How can I encourage speaking, writing, reading, and listening during lab work?

Notes:

Cause-Effect Brainstorming

Gist: Students diagnose a realistic problem by pulling out key ideas and events from text as they read, placing them in a chart.

When to use: During reading, or when diagnosing problems or prompting students to think in terms of cause and effect. Great for CTE classes that teach troubleshooting, including automotive classes and health careers.

The Why

As quick as: 5 minutes

Multiple learning styles:

Scan here for a video discussion of cause-effect graphic organizers.

How It Works

Step 1: Present a situation or problem for students to diagnose, along with text or a video segment that will describe several possible causes of the effect you are discussing.

Step 2: Give students one of the graphic organizers on the next two pages, and have them write the problem or situation being diagnosed in the single box to the right, under the heading "effect." For example, in an automotive class, if the problem was that a client said, "My car hesitates," they would write the client's statement in the "effect" box.

Step 3: Tell students the purpose of their reading or viewing: to identify all the causes of the problem.

Step 4: Allow students time to read quietly for the different causes that connect to this effect. During their reading, they should annotate or take notes of possible causes, and they should circle or jot down relevant vocabulary terms. Instruct them to use specific vocabulary words in the chart.

Step 5: Have students write possible causes in the left-hand column until they have identified 3 or 4.

Step 6: Instruct students to go look again at the possible causes they wrote down. They should then look back at their circled (or listed) associated vocabulary terms and their annotated text. Any notes or ideas that are associated with one of the "possible causes" should be written into the diagram at this point.

Step 7: Bring the class together to discuss the causes and clarify mistakes that they may have made while working on this.

Twist: Once the causes have been discussed, you could quickly partner students and have them rank the causes in order of strongest-to-weakest or most likely. This would require them to get back into the text and look for evidence that some possible causes are more likely than others. Any time students are ranking and justifying, you are pushing them toward more critical, strategic thinking.

Common Core Connection

- Cite textual evidence
  CCSS.ELA-LITERACY.RST.11-12.1
- Analyze how text structures information into categories or hierarchies
  CCSS.ELA-LITERACY.RST.11-12.5
- Integrate and evaluate multiple diverse sources to solve a problem
  CCSS.ELA-LITERACY.RST.11-12.7
- Evaluate hypotheses, data, analysis, and conclusions; verify data and corroborate or challenge conclusions with other evidence
  CCSS.ELA-LITERACY.RST.11-12.8
- Work toward proficient independent understanding of text
  CCSS.ELA-LITERACY.RST.11-12.10

SAMPLE CAUSE & EFFECT CHART - ELECTRICAL

Often when dealing with electricity, one wrong step can create a whole range of problems, from slight to very serious.

Part 1: Think about and write 3 "causes" below dealing with procedures we have discussed—things we could do to create negative "effects." Just write 3 causes. We'll come up with possible "effects" as a class.

CAUSE	EFFECT
1.	
2.	
3.	

But I'm Not a Reading Teacher!

(Electrical Cause-Effect, cont.)

Part 2: Test Your Partner

This time, think in reverse. Make up 3 effects—or things that could happen—without writing anything in the cause boxes. When you and your partner both have listed 3 effects, trade papers to see if you can each think of the CAUSE your partner was thinking of.

CAUSE	EFFECT
1.	
2.	
3.	

SAMPLE CAUSE & EFFECT - AUTOMOTIVE

Often bad driving habits cause premature problems with different parts of a braking system.

Part 1: Create 3 causes from driving habits you can think of, then come up with an "effect" on the brake system.

CAUSE	EFFECT
1.	
2.	
3.	

(Automotive Cause-Effect, cont.)

Part 2: Now collaborate with the student next to you. Make up 3 hypothetical situations that could happen with brake problems and brake repairs. Put a "cause" & an "effect" in the boxes for each of your 3 examples.

CAUSE	EFFECT
1.	
2.	
3.	

Part 2: Productive Talk

Cause and Effect

Name: _____

Title: _____

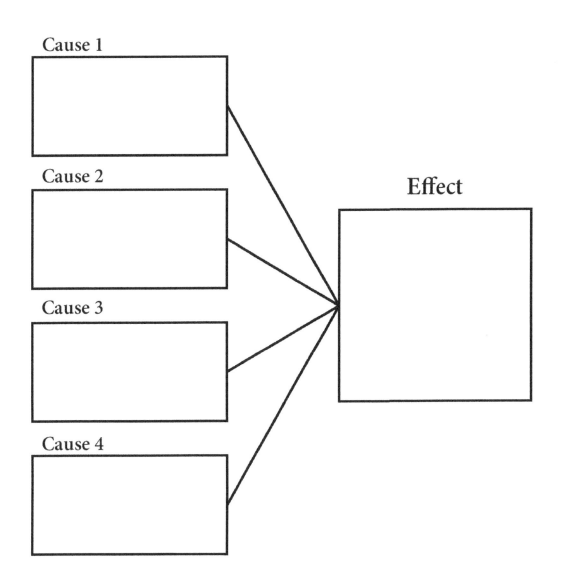

SWOT Analysis (Brainstorming through Different Lenses)

The Why

As quick as: 10 minutes

Multiple learning styles:

Blended learning: If you don't have a written scenario, we suggest finding a 4- to 10-minute video on your topic.

Gist: Students examine the strengths, weaknesses, opportunities, and threats to gain a well-rounded understanding of any idea and evaluate before taking the next step in a process.

When to use: To review for performance testing or to solve a problem (hypothetical or in the lab).

How It Works

Step 1: Divide students into groups or keep the whole class together.

Step 2: Distribute a blank SWOT diagram (like the one on the facing page) to each group, or have students create a large version on the board or on chart paper.

Step 3: Present students with a topic, video clip, or written scenario. For example, show a video of an interaction with a customer.

Step 4: Say, "As a group, analyze the video through 4 different lenses: strengths, weaknesses, opportunities, and threats. Jot down ideas in each box as you go." For a customer interaction video, students would analyze the actions and words of the professional worker and gauge customer satisfaction.

NOTE: Don't feel constrained to the exact terminology on the diagram. For example, if your situation does not include any threats, use the word "tweaks" instead, to help students brainstorm possible changes.

NOTE: If you use a large diagram on the board, have students use Post-it notes to add their ideas to a box. Post-its allow you to move ideas between boxes, and they get students out of their seats to stick them on the board.

Step 5: Lead a group discussion of the positive and negative aspects of the topic. For a customer interaction, challenge students to suggest changes the worker could make.

Twist: Have student groups practice performance testing and record themselves on video. Then have groups trade videos and analyze each other's actions using a SWOT analysis.

Common Core Connection

- Summarize complex concepts by paraphrasing
  CCSS.ELA-LITERACY.RST.11-12.2
- Analyze how text structures information into categories or hierarchies
  CCSS.ELA-LITERACY.RST.11-12.5
- Integrate and evaluate multiple diverse sources to solve a problem
  CCSS.ELA-LITERACY.RST.11-12.7
- Evaluate hypotheses, data, analysis, and conclusions; verify data and corroborate or challenge conclusions with other evidence
  CCSS.ELA-LITERACY.RST.11-12.8
- Synthesize information from various sources into a coherent understanding
  CCSS.ELA-LITERACY.RST.11-12.9
- Work toward proficient independent understanding of text
  CCSS.ELA-LITERACY.RST.11-12.10

SWOT Analysis

S: Strengths	W: Weaknesses
O: Opportunities	**T: Threats**

Choices and Consequences (Brainstorming Possibilities)

Gist: Students use divergent "if-then" thinking to explore possibilities rather than locking into a single answer.

When to use: As a critical-thinking exercise for decision-making. Use with either cooperation or competition to practice divergent thinking.

The Why

As quick as: 15 minutes

Multiple learning styles:

How It Works

Step 1: Give students a scenario that requires them to make a choice. Example: in an EMT class, students answer a hypothetical dispatch call.

Step 2: Students use the organizer on p.143 to record the scenario in the first box. To encourage more collaboration, have student groups create their own version of this organizer.

Step 3: Once students understand the scenario, have them record two possible choices they could make as the next steps and write them in the two center boxes.

Step 4: For each possible choice, students should brainstorm at least two possible consequences. Divergent thinking means exploring many options, so encourage students to think all the way through the possibilities. You may need to model for students how divergent thinking works.

Step 5: Once students have listed four or more consequences, have them go back and decide as a group which are positive and which are negative. Then evaluate as a class and choose the best choice.

Common Core Connection

- Cite textual evidence
  CCSS.ELA-LITERACY.RST.11-12.1
- Summarize complex concepts by paraphrasing
  CCSS.ELA-LITERACY.RST.11-12.2
- Analyze how text structures information into categories or hierarchies
  CCSS.ELA-LITERACY.RST.11-12.5
- Analyze author's purpose and identify unresolved issues
  CCSS.ELA-LITERACY.RST.11-12.6
- Synthesize information from various sources into a coherent understanding
  CCSS.ELA-LITERACY.RST.11-12.9
- Work toward proficient independent understanding of text
  CCSS.ELA-LITERACY.RST.11-12.10

Part 2: Productive Talk

Consequence Chart

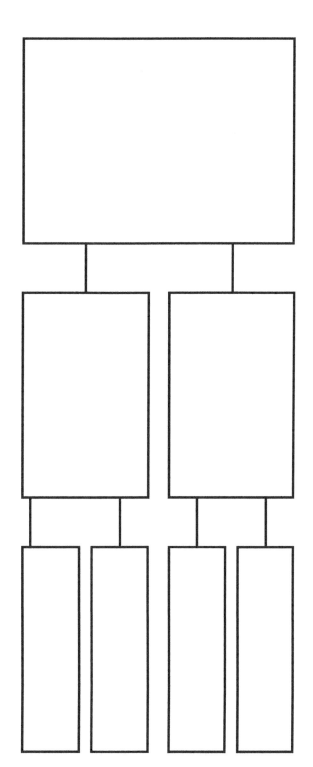

Purpose:
To explore options when making decisions.

Procedure:
Start with a 'what if' questions or problem and write it in the box on the left. Students suggest solutions to be written in the middle boxes and the possible consequences of each solution action in the boxes on the right.

TEACHER ACTIVITY

Try out prediction at your next collaborative teacher meeting. Have your fellow teachers fill out the guide below, or create your own based on whatever topic you plan to discuss. See if discussion improves when everyone has made predictions and considered these ideas ahead of time.

Professional Learning: Feedback

Prediction Guide for Teachers

Directions: For each of the statements below, think about what it says and follow your intuition. If you think the statement is correct, place a check mark on the line. If you think the statement is wrong, just leave it blank.

_____ 1. It is more helpful for students to get corrective feedback than evaluative feedback.

_____ 2. It is not really possible to say that one change in instruction is better than another. It's up to a teacher to decide what changes are most helpful to students.

_____ 3. It is best for students to be tested over material immediately after they learn it.

_____ 4. Students giving feedback to one another can be just as effective as students receiving feedback from their teachers.

_____ 5. It is possible that some feedback, or the way it's delivered, can actually do more harm than good.

After everyone has made their predictions, read the text on the following page, *Research and Theory on Providing Feedback*, then begin a discussion. Note how well prediction techniques improve reading and feedback among your staff. How can you use prediction with students?

Research and Theory on Providing Feedback (Excerpt)

By Sandra Adams

One of the most generalizable strategies a teacher can use is to provide students with feedback on how well they are doing. In fact, feedback seems to work well in so many situations that it led researcher John Hattie (1992) to make the following comment after analyzing almost 8,000 studies:

The most powerful single modification that enhances achievement is feedback. The simplest prescription for improving education must be "dollops of feedback." (p. 9)

We have drawn the following four generalizations to guide the use of feedback:

1. Feedback should be corrective in nature.

Note that some of the effect sizes reported in the data are .90 and even higher. An effect size near .40 is generally considered to be a moderate achievement gain, so .90 is very high. Generally, feedback that produces these large effect sizes is "corrective" in nature. This means that it provides students with an explanation of what they are doing that is correct and what they are doing that is not correct. Perhaps one of the more interesting findings regarding feedback was reported by Bangert-Downs (1991). The overall effect size they reported was only .26. Their study, however, focused on feedback that takes the form of a test or, as they refer to it, "test-like events." The findings from this study show some rather strong implications for education. Notice that simply telling students that their answer on a test is right or wrong has a negative effect on achievement. Providing students with the correct answer has a moderate effect size (.22). The best feedback appears to involve an explanation as to what is accurate and what is inaccurate in terms of student responses. In addition, asking students to keep working on a task until they succeed appears to enhance achievement.

2. Feedback should be timely.

The timing of feedback appears to be critical to its effectiveness. Feedback given immediately after a test-like situation is best. In general, the more delay that occurs in giving feedback, the less improvement there is in achievement. Notice that feedback immediately after a test item has a relatively low average effect size of .19, and providing students with feedback immediately after a test has the largest effect size (.72). Finally, consider the different effects for timing of test-role feedback. Giving tests immediately after a learning situation has a very negligible effect on achievement. Giving a test one day after a learning situation seems to be optimal.

3. Feedback should be specific to a criterion.

For feedback to be most useful, it should reference a specific level of skill or knowledge. A different way of saying this is that feedback should be criterion-referenced, as opposed to norm-referenced. When feedback is norm-referenced, it informs students about where they stand in relationship to other students. This tells students nothing about their learning. Criterion-referenced feedback tells students where they stand relative to a specific target of knowledge or skill.

4. Students can effectively provide some of their own feedback.

We tend to think that providing feedback is something done exclusively by teachers. Research indicates, however, that students can effectively monitor their own progress. Commonly this takes the form of students' simply keeping track of their performance as learning occurs (Linely, 1972). The use of feedback in self-evaluation and self-regulation has been strongly encouraged by researcher Grant Wiggins.

Making It Work – Productive Talk

- In what ways do I see the value of productive talk in my classroom? Is discussion important to CTE students?

- What are the biggest hindrances to good discussion in my class? How can I address them?

- What are some lessons I already teach that could be improved by productive talk?

Notes:

PART 3: DISCIPLINARY LITERACY

IN THIS SECTION:

What is Disciplinary Literacy?

Developing Your Goals for Disciplinary Literacy Instruction

Planning Strategies for Disciplinary Literacy Instruction

What Does Literacy Mean in My Discipline?

Disciplinary Literacy: Big Ideas

    Writing Prompt Carousel
    Specified Summary (Guided Note-Taking)
    Bigwig Bio
    Prediction Guide (Disciplinary Literacy Version)
    Video Close Reading
    Professional Interview

Disciplinary Literacy: Habits of Mind

    Real-World Scenarios
    Career Curator
    Know Your Target Market
    Informational Speech
    Punch the Holes in It
    Reading Schematics, Diagrams, and Blueprints (Text Features)
    Examining Ethics
    Professional Work Ethic

What Is Disciplinary Literacy?

We have discussed the importance of using general literacy skills to improve learning in your CTE classroom—an approach called content area literacy. With content area literacy, you can use general strategies, like those we have shared, to infuse your class with basic literacy skills and improve engagement and learning. But in this section, we want to move beyond the use of general literacy skills and help you go deeper, into disciplinary literacy.

Disciplinary literacy is the specific set of skills and knowledge that characterize expert literacy within a discipline. It is the idea that being literate in general is not quite the same thing as being literate in a specific field. Disciplinary literacy skills are by definition more specific to a field than the basic Speaking, Writing, Reading, and Listening skills we have focused on thus far. They describe exactly *how* an expert speaks, writes, reads, and listens within that field. Therefore, you will need to do more specific planning to adapt and develop instructional strategies for disciplinary literacy in your classroom.

Before you can begin to develop strategies for improving disciplinary literacy instruction, consider the following questions to determine what makes a person literate in your field.

- **What could "text" mean for your discipline?** Is there a large number of journals and websites with which experts are familiar? If not, are video tutorials common? Or instructional manuals?

- **How is language used in your discipline?** Is a particular format, such as APA, required for professional writing in your field? Is text usually formal or colloquial? Does it use active or passive voice? Does it include many words with related roots (such as Latin)? Is word classification important, or is the focus more heavily on making connections between events and ideas? Are there specific words that mean something different in your discipline than they do to the layperson? How important are precision and accuracy in writing or speaking about your work? Is it acceptable to share hypotheses and incomplete ideas, or to share specific data?

- **How do experts in your discipline think about the author/source of a text?** Do they continually look for bias and think about how a source's background may have influenced the content (like a historian)? Are there specific sources that are known to be more reliable and high-quality than others (well-known research labs, websites, etc.)? Is there a governing body with which professionals must be familiar?

- **What actions are most emphasized in your field?** Is it more important to describe phenomena or to make predictions? Do experts spend their time innovating original products or maintaining existing structures?

- **What are the norms between professionals in your field?** Do they speak at conferences or trade shows? Do they publish their work? When reading and interacting within your discipline, are experts normally looking for ways to debate and critique each other's work, or is it the norm to suspend critical analysis?

- **How do experts approach problems in your discipline?** What does an expert know to look for when troubleshooting? Is there an established method of questioning and problem-solving?

In teaching disciplinary literacy, your goal is to make students insiders in the way they speak, write, read, listen, and think. Imagine an expert performing a skill in your discipline. If the expert were thinking aloud while working, what would he or she be saying? What mental processes would he or she go through? A top cosmetologist has something different going on in his brain than a beginner does when he observes hair coloring techniques. An expert mechanic approaches problem-solving on the job differently than an expert graphic designer.

Developing Your Goals for Disciplinary Literacy Instruction

If possible, get in touch with other teachers of your content area, either in your school district or over the internet, and brainstorm answers to the questions we asked above. It will be helpful to have multiple voices in determining your disciplinary literacy goals. The box below includes a list of 14 different thinking processes, so you can consider the types of thinking that are most required in your field.

Redefine Literacy for CTE

To help you determine what it means to be literate in your field, consider the following list of thinking tasks. Which thinking processes are important to experts in your field? Which do they emphasize when they perform tasks and when they speak, write, read, and listen on the job?

14 Thinking Processes

1. Vocabulary concept memorization
2. Prediction
3. Ordering steps in a sequence
4. Identifying cause and effect
5. Synthesizing multiple causes and effects for broad generalization
6. Identifying problems that need solving
7. Creating arguments with evidence to support or refute
8. Comparing and contrasting
9. Raising questions with the intent of challenging assumptions
10. Note-taking—deliberate reading with intent of mastering process, deleting nonessentials, elaborating essentials, and summarizing
11. Creating meaning: making connections and developing relationships
12. Preparing for tests: synthesizing
13. Creating products
14. Paraphrasing and delivering feedback during listening

Consider having your students create a visual diagram or poster that defines disciplinary literacy for your classroom. Scan the QR code to the left to see examples.

Scan the bottom code to view a video discussion of how professionals in various disciplines think differently.

Planning Strategies for Disciplinary Literacy Instruction

In creating strategies for disciplinary literacy instruction, consider a two-pronged approach:

1. Big Ideas

Students must understand your discipline's core concepts, driving questions, and key influences.

2. Habits of Mind

Students must practice reasoning, problem-solving, speaking, questioning, and writing in the way that is normative for your discipline.

The Institute for Learning at the University of Pittsburgh has defined disciplinary literacy using these two categories (Bickley, 2014). We find it is easier to understand disciplinary literacy when we consider both "big ideas" and "habits of mind." The rest of Part 3 includes activities to inspire you toward developing disciplinary literacy in your students, and we have organized these activities

---

Metacognition in Disciplinary Literacy

Since literacy within a discipline includes thinking like an expert, it's important for students to notice and evaluate their own thought processes. When students zoom out and assess their thinking, they can try out new approaches and adopt the thinking styles of experts in their field. Encourage metacognition by asking students to explain their thinking and to determine the likely thought process of any author or expert they encounter.

What Does Literacy Mean in My Discipline?

Use this page for notes and ideas as you collaborate with other teachers in your department.

Disciplinary Literacy: Big Ideas

IN THIS SECTION

Writing Prompt Carousel
Specified Summary (Guided Note-Taking)
Bigwig Bio
Prediction Guide (Disciplinary Literacy Version)
Video Close Reading
Professional Interview

The activities in this subgroup help students develop an understanding of the discipline's core concepts, driving questions, and key influences.

You can't simply implement a lesson as it is written for another group of students in another discipline. Disciplinary literacy doesn't work that way. Instead, use these activities as a starting point to help you define the important big ideas in your own discipline, and to inspire lessons that convey those ideas to your students.

- What are the essential questions, big ideas, and driving forces in my discipline? What makes my discipline relevant? Who or what influences it?

Notes:

Writing Prompt Carousel

Gist: Students collaborate in pre-writing by adding new ideas to writing prompts posted throughout the room.

When to use: When helping students to prepare their professional mission statements, philosophies, or portfolios; great for helping students understand the driving questions of your field.

The Why

As quick as: 20 minutes

Multiple learning styles:

How It Works

Step 1: Post 4-5 large sheets of paper around the room, with plenty of space between them. On each paper, write a different question or statement that drives professionals in your field.

Step 2: Divide your students into 4-5 teams, and give each team a different colored marker. Each group begins at a different one of the posted questions.

Step 3: Set a timer for two minutes (or other amount of time). Instruct students as follows: "When I say go, you will have two minutes as a group to write as many ideas as you can that relate to the question. When I call time, every group will take their marker and rotate to the left, just like a carousel."

Step 4: When groups rotate, instruct students as follows: "Before you write anything on your new question, read what the other group(s) wrote. If you disagree with something they have written, put one line through that statement and write a response to it. Then begin to post your own additional thoughts."

Step 5: Continue rotating until all groups have responded to every question. Then facilitate a class discussion. Have students take notes during this discussion.

Step 6: Now students have notes and ideas to help them structure a professional mission statement or philosophy.

Student Perspective: "I had no clue how to come up with my own professional philosophy. Brainstorming through the driving questions helped me, not only to write a great mission statement, but also to begin thinking like a teacher."

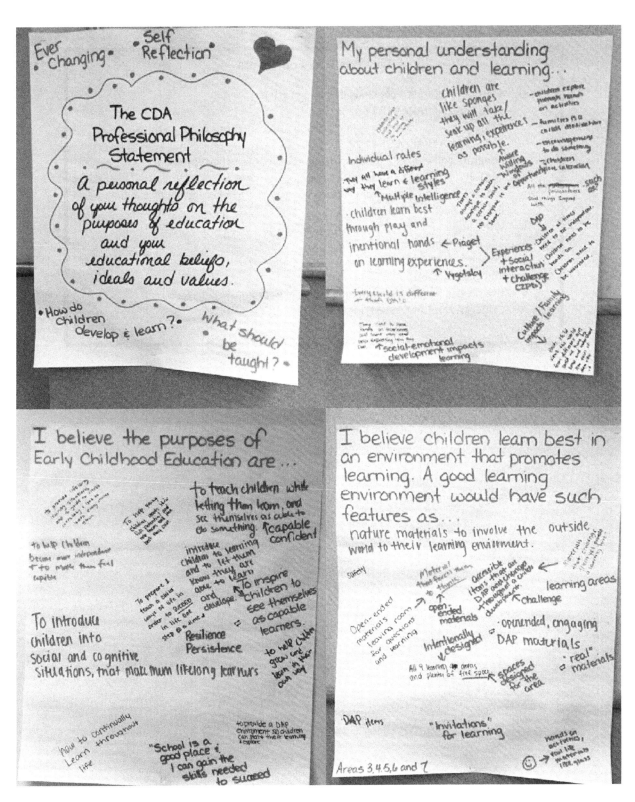

Students in Kim Swain's early childhood education class use the Writing Prompt Carousel to collaboratively brainstorm before writing their educational mission statements for their portfolios.

But I'm Not a Reading Teacher!

Common Core Connection

- Summarize complex concepts by paraphrasing
  CCSS.ELA-LITERACY.RST.11-12.2
- Analyze how text structures information into categories or hierarchies
  CCSS.ELA-LITERACY.RST.11-12.5
- Integrate and evaluate multiple diverse sources to solve a problem
  CCSS.ELA-LITERACY.RST.11-12.7
- Synthesize information from various sources into a coherent understanding
  CCSS.ELA-LITERACY.RST.11-12.9
- Write arguments focused on discipline-specific content
  CCSS.ELA-LITERACY.WHST.11-12.1
- Develop the topic thoroughly
  CCSS.ELA-LITERACY.WHST.11-12.2B
- Use precise language and domain-specific vocabulary
  CCSS.ELA-LITERACY.WHST.11-12.2D

Possible writing prompts I could use in my class:

WRITING AS A THINKING AND PLANNING TOOL

In many CTE disciplines, writing skills may not seem very important at first. But consider how professionals may use writing as a tool for thinking and planning. Instead of producing a newspaper article or writing a book, professionals in CTE disciplines might produce websites, menus, marketing materials, and public service announcements. They might also use writing to plan problem-solving procedures, to take notes, to record their ideas during troubleshooting, or to prepare a speech to other professionals.

Determine how writing is used in your field—formal or informal, as a personal tool or a public communication—and translate those uses into your classroom. Here are a few possibilities:

- Recording procedures
- Producing instruction manuals
- Planning a presentation or demonstration
- Planning for creating a video
- Composing text for a website, poster, or other marketing material
- Creating and filling out invoices
- Drafting legal terms and company policies

- Do I shy away from using writing assignments in my class? Why?

- How can I assign writing that is specific to my discipline, instead of the typical ELA essay?

Notes:

SAMPLE WRITING ASSIGNMENT AND RUBRIC

For further guidance in creating writing assignments, review the following pages for a sample of one automotive teacher's reflective writing assignment and rubric.

Brake, Steering, & Suspension

Writing Assignment

TOPIC: What have you learned so far this semester?

I want you to go beyond surface thinking with this. Think deeper about what you have really learned in this course so far. Explain to me what you have learned by including some of the following points as you write:

- How has your learning connected to what you already knew coming into this course?
- What are some specific examples of things you've learned?
- How has learning in the lab been different than learning in the classroom?
- Was there anything we learned that was different than you thought it would be—clear up misunderstandings?
- Can you describe any moments or activities that you know helped you to learn?

I expect to read this and have a good understanding of where you are in your depth of learned. This will need to be typed.

Follow this guide!

Writing Rubric

Criteria	____ points UNSATISFACTORY Your written work does NOT meet the criteria described	____ points SATISFACTORY Written work meets or exceeds the criteria
1. The prompt is answered completely.		
2. Student uses full sentences and grammar is acceptable. Paper is typed.		
3. Student work demonstrates full understanding by student (details, connections, and /or examples are used if needed).		

Part 3: Disciplinary Literacy

Comments: Total Score: _____

Objective: Reflect on what YOU have learned so far this semester about brakes and the automotive program. Create a persuasive writing to show me what you have learned specifically and how you KNOW you have LEARNED.

Use this rubric to help you organize your thoughts and write with persuasion. CONVINCE me you understand that you've learned some specific things. Follow the rubric to see how your writing will be scored.

Criteria	15-10 points	9-0 points
Organization	Your thoughts are organized and follow a logical sequence. You give evidence with every point you list as to what you have learned about brakes.	Your writing lacks some organization or is difficult to read. You fail to give solid or any evidence to illustrate how you know you've learned key concepts or understandings.
Content	Your writing makes sense to the teacher. The content is specific to our taught content this semester and reflects mastery of the subject. The teacher is able to use the details of the writing to imagine what is being described.	Your writing is confusing or is about content different than what we have studied in the classroom and the lab. Your writing lacks in detail and doesn't create any clear picture in the mind of the reader.
Craftsmanship	My paper is neat and easy to read. Contains at least 3 body paragraphs and a strong concluding paragraph that has 5-7 sentences.	My paper is low quality, writing with poor penmanship, or is messy in general—lacking professionalism. The paper is not divided into paragraphs or too short in length.
Mechanics	All of my punctuation, spelling, and capitalizations are correct. My grammar is correct throughout the whole paper.	Paper contains numerous mistakes and misspellings. Incorrect grammar.

Specified Summary (Guided Note-Taking)

"My students don't seem to know how to take notes they can actually use in this field!"

Gist: Text (or other activity) is broken down into sections, which students periodically summarize with a very limited number of words. They practice evaluating and prioritizing information according to its importance in the career field, as well as re-wording it for understanding, all while they read or listen.

When to Use: During reading/listening/watching a demonstration, when your students need a structure for engaging with the material or haven't learned to take good notes on their own. Especially useful when the material contains new vocabulary words and concepts.

The Why

As quick as: 5 minutes

Multiple learning styles:

Secondary educators often get frustrated with a student's lack of note-taking skill. Eliminate frustration and equip them for learning by proactively teaching note-taking.

How It Works

Step 1: If your text (or activity) is longer than about a page, or very complex, chunk it ahead of time.

Step 2: Explain the purpose to students, "We are going to practice a skill that will help you to read (listen) actively. Taking good notes requires you to decide quickly which information is important to your future career and record it efficiently, limited by time and space. I want your notes to be helpful to you both in understanding now and when you review them later."

Step 3: Say, "We will read this section silently (or watch this demonstration, etc.), and afterwards you will write a 16-word summary in your notes. It must be exactly 16 words, so you may have to get clever." (As the teacher, you can choose any number or type of limit. The important thing is that students learn to eliminate unnecessary words while identifying big ideas and writing directly.)

Step 4: Let students begin reading or participating in the class activity. Once they start writing their summaries, walk around the room to see who is struggling, offering guiding questions where needed.

Step 5: Your next step depends on your goals for your students:
  Option A. If you want a quiet, reflective reading time that allows students to work at their own pace, continue the activity as before, allowing students to move on to the next section and write another limited summary (Tip: choose a different number of words this

time!). This option gives you a chance to spend more time assisting students who need help.

Option B. Randomly select a few of the summaries to write on the board. Facilitate a discussion of the summaries using pre-written questions before moving on to the next section of text/listening. Challenge students to give evidence for why their main points are relevant to the career field.

Option C. Have students turn to a person near them and compare their summaries. Allow them a few minutes to discuss and then begin reading the next section. After this reading, have the partners write a specified summary together. This allows you to create a type of think-pair-share lesson for the class.

Student Perspective: "I've learned how to take notes that will be useful when I study, and along the way I've compiled statements that help me sum up the big ideas of the field."

Common Core Connection

- Summarize complex concepts by paraphrasing
  CCSS.ELA-LITERACY.RST.11-12.2
- Determine meaning of key terms as used in context
  CCSS.ELA-LITERACY.RST.11-12.4
- Analyze author's purpose and identify unresolved issues
  CCSS.ELA-LITERACY.RST.11-12.6
- Integrate and evaluate multiple diverse sources to solve a problem
  CCSS.ELA-LITERACY.RST.11-12.7
- Synthesize information from various sources into a coherent understanding
  CCSS.ELA-LITERACY.RST.11-12.9
- Work toward proficient independent understanding of text
  CCSS.ELA-LITERACY.RST.11-12.10
- Use precise language and domain-specific vocabulary
  CCSS.ELA-LITERACY.WHST.11-12.2D

Variation: Sketch Notes

Give your students the tools and freedom to make their notes their own with visual notetaking. For sketch noting methods, check out the fascinating videos by Doug Neill of VerbalToVisual.com. If you're not into drawing, you can still harness the power of visual notetaking. Scan the code below to see how.

Taking notes in this way isn't about making the notes look pretty. It's about what happens in the brain when you take sketch notes. By paying attention to text weight, layout, connecting lines, and white space, you engage your brain in sorting, evaluating, organizing information, and analyzing relationships all while taking notes!

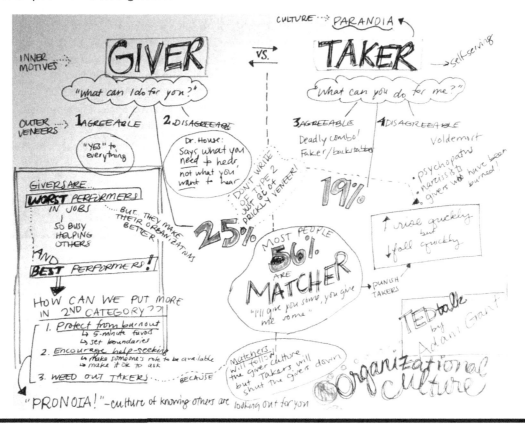

Here's a photo of sketch notes we took while listening to a TED Talk by Adam Grant.

Scan below for Doug Neill's Verbal To Visual video.

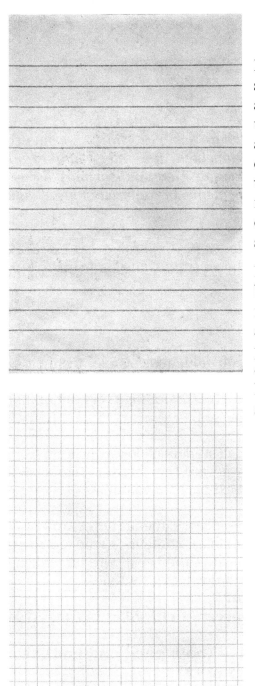

Stick to a System – Any System

If professionals in your discipline commonly use a specific method for planning and note-taking, such as a favorite app, introduce it and encourage students to use it to take notes during class. However, when there are no specific industry standards or norms, encourage students to experiment and use the tools that make it easy for them to stick with an organized note-taking system. Provide a basic folder, notebook, or binder for storage and organization, and let students make it their own.

Note-taking may seem like a basic or obvious skill, but it takes practice. Let your students try a variety of methods and use what works for them. Note-taking apps, loose-leaf lined paper, bound notebooks, graph paper, steno pads, colored pens, highlighters, and even voice memos during lab work may come in handy. The important thing is that the notes serve the student.

Bigwig Bio

"I want students to know the influential people in my field, but we don't have time for long research projects!"

Gist: Students introduce an influential "bigwig" to a classmate or small group using a short, 3-sentence structure that communicates the most important information about the person. Then small groups discuss possible future advancements or repercussions of the person's work.

When to use: When there's no time for a big research project, to give historical context to developments within a specific field.

The Why

As quick as: 20 minutes

Metacognition (thinking about thinking): As students determine which information to include in their bare-bones introduction, they are rationalizing. As they discuss afterward, and especially if they rank the bigwigs' contributions by importance to the field, they must explain their thought process.

Multiple learning styles:

Focus on process: This activity provides choice, reducing the need for grades as a motivator. It includes multiple steps, allowing you to assess understanding informally, without grades.

How It Works

Step 1: Generate a list of influential people, technology developments, or organizations in your field. Have students brainstorm this list, or for a very unfamiliar topic, provide the list yourself.

Step 2: *Select a topic.* Each student chooses one item from the list and finds out who are the "bigwigs" associated with that item. See the next page for examples.

Step 3: *Conduct short research.* Either as homework or in class (if internet is available), students spend up to 10 minutes researching, with the goal of prioritizing information and boiling it down to 3 sentences:
1. **Who is this person?**
2. **What was the career field like before this person's work?**
3. **What has happened (both good and bad) as a result of this person's work?**

The goal is not a comprehensive understanding, but simply a general overview. This 3-sentence structure will help your students improve both their writing skills and their knowledge of important people in your field.

> **Common Core Connection**
>
> - Explain how individuals, ideas, and events interact and develop
>   CCSS.ELA-LITERACY.RI.11-12.3
> - Analyze how an "author" uses and refines a key term
>   CCSS.ELA-LITERACY.RI.11-12.4
> - Determine the point of view or purpose of an "author"
>   CCSS.ELA-LITERACY.RI.11-12.6
> - Summarize and paraphrase in simpler but accurate terms
>   CCSS.ELA-LITERACY.RST.11-12.2
> - Conduct short research projects, narrowing the inquiry and synthesizing multiple sources
>   CCSS.ELA-LITERACY.W.11-12.7

Step 4: *Introduce the Bigwig*. Either the next day or after in-class research time, group students in twos or threes. They each get less than a minute to introduce an influential Bigwig to their small group in three sentences. The bigwig could be a name that was on the list, or it could be a person they uncovered when they researched their item from the list.

Twist: Assign multiple students to introduce the same "bigwig." After independent in-class research, it would be interesting to compare and contrast each student's take on the work of the same person.

Twist 2: In groups of 3 or 4, students should introduce their bigwig, then rank the 3 or 4 bigwigs by the importance of their contribution to the field. Use the strategy of forced agreement, requiring groups to discuss and argue with evidence until everyone agrees. Then share their ranking with the whole class. Prompt students to explain what makes one contribution more important than another (i.e. long-term use, widespread impact, leading to other significant ideas, etc.).

Student Perspective: Bigwig Bio gave me a snapshot of how the field has advanced and helped me learn how to think about the future of this career field. And the discussion was much more interesting than a lecture!"

Bigwig Bio Examples

Cosmetology: "Florence Nightingale Graham, known in business as Elizabeth Arden, created the concept of the makeover. Before she sold cosmetics and performed makeovers, makeup was often associated with lower classes and prostitutes. As a result of her work, makeup became proper for "ladylike" women, and the cosmetics industry has fixated on makeovers ever since."

Medical science class: "Alexander Fleming discovered penicillin in 1928, which became the first antibiotic. Before this discovery, people often died from bacterial infections. His work—alongside Doctors Howard Florey, Ernst Chain, and Norman Heatley—has saved many lives led to antibiotics being commonplace, but it has also enabled them to be overprescribed and created new strains of bacteria."

IT class: "Larry Page and Sergey Brin are co-founders of Google and the inventors of PageRank, an algorithm that ranks websites in Google's search engine results. Before they created Google, finding information on the internet was not efficient. Their work has made it fast and easy to find information, but it has also created a hierarchy in websites, giving popular sites priority and making it hard for small sites to be found."

Bigwig Bio Follow-Up Lesson Idea: Up-and-Comers

Inspire students by showing them others who have found creative niche markets for their skills. After discussing "bigwigs" who have forged new paths, introduce some "up-and-comers" who are beginning to change the industry. Or challenge students to find examples on their own. In a construction class you might show students this linked article from This Old House (top).

This kind of lesson could be a first step toward a student's staying current and informed on new developments in a career field, which is part of disciplinary literacy. It could also inspire students to find their own way to use the skills you are teaching.

Scan the bottom code to see CheatSheet.com's list of 13 jobs with the fastest-growing salaries (Many of them are CTE-related careers). The idea is to share articles like this with your students and introduce them to practical sources of career-related reading materials that will help them consider their own futures.

Making It Work: Bigwig Bio

- Which historical figures influenced the development of this field?

- Which current influencers lead the field, and why should my students learn about them?

- Who are some up-and-comers in this career field, and how might I introduce creative career paths to my students?

Notes:

Prediction Guide (Disciplinary Literacy Version)

(See Prediction Guide (vocabulary version) in part 1. Both adapted from Mark A. Forget, Ph. D's "Anticipation Guide.")

"I wish students would stop just skimming text to find the answer!"

Gist: Students read prepared statements rephrased from a text (video, audio presentation), including statements an expert in your field would or would not say. Students choose whether they agree or disagree. They discuss and explain their choices, then they read/view/listen and note their correct or incorrect predictions. Afterwards, they discuss again and reach consensus.

When to use: Before and during any reading, viewing, or listening activity, to engage students with prediction and help them think like an expert. Great for any CTE class.

The Why

As quick as: 30 minutes

Multiple learning styles:

How It Works

Step 1 (before class): Create a prediction guide for the day's reading assignment, video or audio presentation, or in-class demonstration. You can create an anticipation guide for virtually any "text." Here's how:

Read or watch the text or activity, looking for the most important terms you want students to learn from it. Then, for each of those terms, write one related statement, reworded from the text. **It is important that you reword the statements because your goal is for students to construct meaning themselves, not simply hunt for correct answers.** Each statement should be plausible, and some statements should be complex, vague, overly broad, or controversial. Include some statements that contain information from multiple sections of the text, so that students must interpret the text broadly rather than picking out answers. Some statements may be correct, some may be incorrect, and others may not have a correct answer. Vocabulary terms should be bolded or underlined on the anticipation guide. Example statement (construction class): It is illegal in the U.S. to call yourself an **architect** unless you are licensed by a state. (This is true.)

Step 2 (in class): Introduce prediction. Explain that strategic thinkers naturally make predictions and keep their predictions in mind while reading or listening. Emphasize that predictions do not have to be right—either way, they give a purpose for reading and help make it more interesting. You may even introduce the idea of prediction by modeling:

"I'm betting 75% of you posted to Twitter over the weekend." Then ask for a show of hands and explain how you're much more invested in the answer after having made a prediction.

Step 3: Students read the statements individually and connect each statement to prior knowledge, predicting whether the statement will prove to be correct. Students mark "correct" statements with a checkmark. Remind students that they are looking for statements that an expert would say.

Step 4: Students connect with an elbow-partner, discussing each person's response to each statement and attempting to reach a consensus by explaining their logic and prior knowledge to each other. The teacher should move around the room, monitoring discussions and checking for prior knowledge.

Step 5: Students read the text (silently or with their partner), seeking evidence to back up or refute their predictions. For a video or audio presentation, students should watch or listen, making note on their anticipation guide when evidence is given. Students should note all evidence that relates to a statement, even conflicting evidence. Modification: for low-level readers, you may want to group them together and read aloud, reading a statement yourself and then having them read it back to you before discussion.

Step 6: Students return to their partner or a small group to discuss their evidence. Their goal is to reach a consensus about all the statements AND all the logical evidence for their statements.

Step 7: Teacher leads a whole-group discussion in which students share and defend the statements they agree with, eventually coming up with an agreed-upon list of "expert statements." Encourage argument between students, and encourage students to probe into each other's reasoning as they question each other's positions.

 Scan the QR code to the left to access sample anticipation guides for various CTE disciplines.

> **Common Core Connection**
>
> - Cite textual evidence
>   CCSS.ELA-LITERACY.RST.11-12.1
> - Determine meaning of key terms as used in context
>   CCSS.ELA-LITERACY.RST.11-12.4
> - Integrate and evaluate multiple diverse sources to solve a problem
>   CCSS.ELA-LITERACY.RST.11-12.7
> - Evaluate hypotheses, data, analysis, and conclusions; verify data and corroborate or challenge conclusions with other evidence
>   CCSS.ELA-LITERACY.RST.11-12.8
> - Synthesize information from various sources into a coherent understanding
>   CCSS.ELA-LITERACY.RST.11-12.9
> - Work toward proficient independent understanding of text
>   CCSS.ELA-LITERACY.RST.11-12.10
> - Use precise language and domain-specific vocabulary
>   CCSS.ELA-LITERACY.WHST.11-12.2D

Sample prediction guide
Used with text about the TV industry

What you already know about the TV Industry?
Anticipation Guide

* Directions: For each of the statements below, use a   to mark if YOU believe the statement is correct. If you think the statement is false, simply leave the line blank.

This is not for a grade---We'll get the right answers together.

_____ 1. The future of the television industry is highly connected to the future of digital technology.

_____2. Televisions were first watched in American homes during the 1950s decade, with VCRs following in the 1970s.

_____3. When satellite broadcast technology became available, it really didn't change the television industry much at all.

_____4. Nearly all cable television produced comes from broadcast and satellite today.

_____ 5. Commercial broadcast television simply means that consumers do not have to pay to watch the programs.

_____6. Television networks must create, bundle, and sell all of their own television programming to consumers like you and I.

_____7. NBC & CBS are such large networks that they each have 100s of affiliate stations connected to them.

_____8. A brand new sitcom or drama series can immediately be syndicated to other networks.

_____9. Last year, a 30-second spot (commercial) during the Super Bowl was as high as $3 million!

_____10. Demonstrating the competitive nature of the television industry, this year the NFL has decided that the Super Bowl half-time performer will actually have to pay the NFL in order to perform.

_____11. Your family could actually be selected at some point to serve as a Nielsen group, and help rank shows by how good/entertaining they are.

_____12. Technology and Innovation are the driving forces of the television industry.

Making It Work – Prediction Guide

- How would an expert in my discipline look at the facts to make a prediction? How can I teach that process to my students?

- What are some texts (including videos, websites, trade magazine selections, professional journal articles, etc.) I could use to create prediction guides for my students?

Notes:

But I'm Not a Reading Teacher!

Video Close Reading

"How can my students become active participants and questioners during an instructional video?"

Gist: Students use informational videos (we suggest the free website EDpuzzle.com) that are broken down into chunks and combined with a corresponding text. Throughout the activity, students periodically annotate, paraphrase, summarize, and discuss the text and video.

When to use: As an engaging form of close reading, when students need to understand informational text because of its importance to their future careers. This activity will help students learn to chunk text, to read and think critically, and to actively question as they work through information.

The Why

As quick as: 45 minutes

Multiple learning styles:

How It Works

Step 1: Visit EDpuzzle.com or another video source, and find a video that relates to your subject. EDpuzzle contains a wealth of practical videos for career and technology classes. For example, for a medical class, you might choose a video about HIPAA privacy issues.

Step 2: Choose a corresponding text, perhaps a difficult or dry text that your students might struggle to read on their own. It could be a selection from your textbook or an important document used in your career field. For the video on HIPAA privacy issues, you might use an actual HIPAA agreement. Provide a copy of the text for each student to read as they watch the video.

Step 3: Using the EDpuzzle site, tailor your video so that it includes several breaks (at least 3 or 4). We want to "chunk" the watching and reading to create time for students to interact with the material. You can insert questions, prompts, and corresponding parts of your text into the video during these breaks. Refer to the structure in Step 4 as a guide for prepping the video.

Step 4: Implement the lesson using the following structure as a guide:

- Before the video begins: Group students as partners or small groups. Students read the text once to themselves. Say, "Now as we watch this video, refer back to your copy of the text as you watch. Whenever you hear unfamiliar words or technical terms in the video, underline them in the text and make a note of any details from the video that give clues to their meaning."
- **Break 1: Annotation.** Guide the students as they annotate the text, noting details from the video that correspond to the text. Allow them to collaborate with their partners and share details they noticed.

> You can use the four-break process to guide you in chunking any video, reading, or lab activity:
>
> 1. Annotation/noting details
> 2. Paraphrasing
> 3. Questioning
> 4. Summarizing

- **Break 2: Paraphrasing.** Take this break after a complicated or very technical part of the video. Challenge students to identify something in the text that corresponds to this part of the video. Then challenge them to explain that part in their own words to a partner. (You may want to do multiple paraphrasing breaks so that both partners get a chance to paraphrase new information. Create a paraphrasing break anytime there is complex information.)
- **Break 3: Questioning.** Create a designated break in the video for students to write down a question that relates to the text. It can be a question they don't know the answer to, a response to something a partner said during paraphrasing, or it could be a hypothetical question for further discussion. For example, in the HIPAA example, a student might ask, "What would happen if someone hacked into a patient's online medical records?"
- **Break 4 (at the end of the video): Summarizing.** Student pairs or groups should take a few minutes to collaboratively write a short summary of the video and text (you may specifically limit them to 3 sentences or so).

Twist: EDpuzzle allows you to create many different lessons that students can work on individually or with a group. Follow the structure above (chunking for annotation, paraphrasing, questioning, and summarizing), and during the breaks introduce lessons created on the site to go along with the video.

> **Common Core Connection**
>
> - Cite textual evidence
>   CCSS.ELA-LITERACY.RST.11-12.1
> - Summarize complex concepts by paraphrasing
>   CCSS.ELA-LITERACY.RST.11-12.2
> - Follow a complex multi-step procedure; analyze results based on text
>   CCSS.ELA-LITERACY.RST.11-12.3
> - Determine meaning of key terms as used in context
>   CCSS.ELA-LITERACY.RST.11-12.4
> - Analyze how text structures information into categories or hierarchies
>   CCSS.ELA-LITERACY.RST.11-12.5
> - Analyze author's purpose and identify unresolved issues
>   CCSS.ELA-LITERACY.RST.11-12.6
> - Work toward proficient independent understanding of text
>   CCSS.ELA-LITERACY.RST.11-12.10

Professional Interview

The Gist: students interview a professional in your field.

When to use: when students need a practical understanding of the discipline, to consider their personal future career path.

The Why

As quick as: extended

Multiple learning styles:

How It Works

Step 1: Challenge students to find a professional in your field who will sit down with them for a short interview. If possible, provide them with names and contact information of local businesses, and discuss how they should speak to whoever answers the phone. Encourage students to set up an in-person interview if possible, but if they struggle to find an interviewee, remind them of the possibilities of phone and e-mail.

Step 2: Spend some time in class brainstorming interview questions that are relevant to the person's career trajectory and the driving questions of your discipline. Allow students to role-play as practice for their interviews. This is an excellent opportunity to practice norms for professional communication in your field.

Step 3: After students have completed their interviews, facilitate a time of sharing what they've learned in class.

Student Perspective: "I feel like I've made a future connection and practiced interacting like an adult professional."

On the next page, you'll find an example of this assignment written out for a culinary class.

Common Core Connection

- Follow a complex multi-step procedure; analyze results based on text
  CCSS.ELA-LITERACY.RST.11-12.3
- Determine meaning of key terms as used in context
  CCSS.ELA-LITERACY.RST.11-12.4
- Synthesize information from various sources into a coherent understanding
  CCSS.ELA-LITERACY.RST.11-12.9
- Use precise language and domain-specific vocabulary
  CCSS.ELA-LITERACY.WHST.11-12.2D

Be a Connector

Part of your value as a CTE teacher is in the connection you provide to the working world. Seek relationships with local professionals who may be willing to speak to your students, and whom students may later call upon when they are seeking internships and entry-level jobs.

Part 3: Disciplinary Literacy

The Professional Interview

- Select an Interviewee candidate from an area restaurant, preferably a manager or assistant manager, but we will accept an employee.
- Name of Interviewee: _____
- Date of Interview: _____
- Signature: _____
- Restaurant Affiliation: _____
- How long has interviewee been employed here? _____

Interview Steps:

1. After you have read Chapter 3, design 12 -14 questions that pertain to this chapter that you will ask during your interview.
2. Choose a restaurant to call and ask the manager or assistant manager for an interview. If you cannot reach someone within 2 days, let us know so that we can help connect you with someone.
3. Conduct the interview and ask your questions. You need to do this verbally. Do NOT simply hand over your list of questions.
4. Take good notes on what your professional contact says and ask for copies of any sanitation guidelines they use with their employee training. Do they use any websites, etc. for training?
5. Put together your interview and design how you will present your interview to the class.
    a. You can present a written paper and give a brief verbal overview of the interview.
    b. You can create visuals (power point or posters) and describe the interview in detail.
6. The interview must reflect chapter 3. Your presentation to teachers and class must reflect your interview AND your understanding of Chapter 3 content and skill development.
7. Interviews must be conducted by: _____
8. Interviews will be presented in class: _____

But I'm Not a Reading Teacher!

Disciplinary Literacy: Habits of Mind

IN THIS SECTION:

Real-World Scenarios
Career Curator
Know Your Target Market
Informational Speech
Punch the Holes in It
Reading Schematics, Diagrams, and Blueprints (Text Features)
Examining Ethics
Professional Work Ethic

> **Immersion in Disciplinary Literacy**
>
> Just like learning a foreign language, learning the mental habits of a discipline requires immersion. Make your classroom a place where the "language" of your field is spoken exclusively, and bring real-world experience into your lessons as often as possible.

The following activities help students practice reading, reasoning, problem-solving, speaking, questioning, and writing in the way that is normative for a specific discipline.

Use these activities as a starting point to help you define the important habits of mind in your own discipline, and to inspire lessons that develop those habits in your students.

- What are the most important habits of mind that characterize an expert in my discipline?

Real-World Scenarios

"I literally just taught this concept! Why aren't they putting it into practice?"

Gist: Provide student groups with hypothetical real-world situations in which they must develop a plan of action the way an expert would.

When to use: To translate theory into practice, to apply concepts you have been teaching to a practical experience before moving on to a new concept, or to check for prior knowledge before beginning a unit.

The Why

As quick as: 10 minutes

Multiple learning styles:

How It Works

Step 1: Present small groups of students with a written scenario and/or images. Scan the QR code to the right to access free printable scenarios for various CTE disciplines. You can also create your own.

Step 2: Instruct students first to break down the issue in the way an expert in your field would, analyzing the parts of the problem. (For example, students ask "why" before "how," finding reasons for the situation's development before making a plan.)

Step 3: Students should create a list of resources available to them in the hypothetical situation, and additional resources needed.

Step 4: As a small group, students should develop a step-by-step plan for solving the problem.

Step 5. Each group should share their plan, either with the whole class or with the teacher, explaining their plan specifically in terms of the theories they have learned in class. Have students point out how their plan exemplifies specific habits of mind that are desirable in your field. (You can also reinforce vocabulary here: "Be sure to use at least six of our vocabulary terms in your explanation.")

Twist: Have students create a video or slideshow, turning their action plan into a safety procedure PSA or instructional material for beginner-level students in the same field.

Twist 2: Create a live-action scenario in which students must act out their solution, and record it on video. Then have students watch, critique, and discuss the recording.

Part 3: Disciplinary Literacy

Twist 3: Scenario notecards – For a single scenario, write various approaches on notecards, using a first-person account. (In a culinary class, some notecards might say, "I want to start a restaurant...I plan on pricing each item by multiplying raw cost by 65%" while others might say, "I'm starting a restaurant...I'll figure out pricing by comparing to a successful restaurant close by." See photo below. In this case, the teacher wants students to learn the five theories on menu pricing in an exploratory way rather than through lecture.) Make several notecards of each account, and distribute them to the class. Everyone who has approach A is in one group, everyone who has B is in another group, etc. Groups should dissect the person's words to figure out their thinking, then discuss. Have students decide which notecards best display an expert's approach.

Student Perspective: "Making a practical plan for the situation helped me make sense of the technical language and apply it like an expert. Justifying my plan to the class helped me understand my thought process and adopt the mental habits of my discipline."

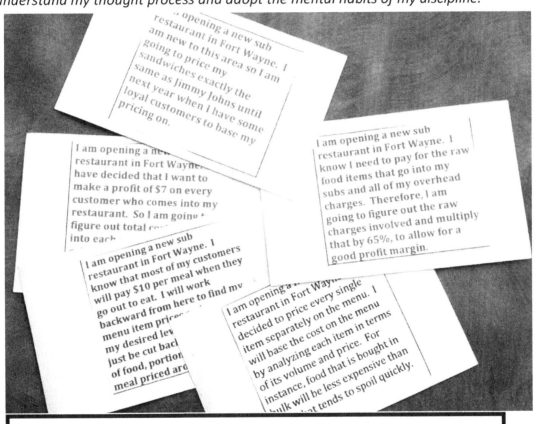

Common Core Connection

- Follow a complex multi-step procedure; analyze results based on text
  CCSS.ELA-LITERACY.RST.11-12.3
- Integrate and evaluate multiple diverse sources to solve a problem
  CCSS.ELA-LITERACY.RST.11-12.7
- Work toward proficient independent understanding of text
  CCSS.ELA-LITERACY.RST.11-12.10
- Use precise language and domain-specific vocabulary
  CCSS.ELA-LITERACY.WHST.11-12.2D

Career Curator

"My students don't seem to think reading is relevant to this career field."

Gist: Students find and organize reading/viewing materials that could replace or supplement portions of the textbook. Students essentially create a classroom media center containing relevant materials that interest them and can later be read and studied by students independently or as part of future in-class assignments. The materials they collect also serve to introduce them to the publications and larger conversation in their chosen career field.

When to use: As a project for the whole class to introduce a topic, or as an enrichment activity for students who are ahead of their peers. This could be an ongoing project that you continue throughout the year.

The Why

As quick as: extended

Focus on process: Multiple steps allow you to assess understanding informally. The practical purpose of creating a trove of resources, combined with autonomy, reduces the need for grades as a motivator.

Multiple learning styles:

How It Works

Step 1: Designate a bookshelf or corner of your classroom to this project.

Step 2: Assign topics. Use your textbook's Table of Contents and chapter sub-headings as a guide, assigning a specific topic or chapter to each student or small group, or working throughout the year, chapter by chapter. To introduce a new unit, ask students to bring in media that is relevant to that topic.

Step 3: Give students a list of places to look to get them started, such as technical journals, websites, histories, manuals, and magazines related to your field, but encourage them to bring in anything interesting that relates to the topic. They may also find historical illustrations, diagrams, and photographs online by searching for public domain photographs.

Step 4: Organize it. Provide blank labels and shelf space, and allow students working in groups to create categories and subcategories for the materials they have collected. Give them the freedom to arrange media and artifacts in a way that makes sense to them, and allow plenty of time for this part. As they organize, they will need to explain to each other what each piece of media is about and determine how items relate to one another. They should also be able to explain to you and other classmates how it is organized and how to find what they are looking for.

Step 5: Allow students to borrow items from your new career-field media center, and refer to it when choosing texts for future lessons and projects.

Common Core Connection

- Determining and summarizing the central idea of a text/piece of media/artifact
  CCSS.ELA-LITERACY.RST.11-12.2
- Analyzing how categories are structured, both within the class textbook and within the media center as a whole.
  CCSS.ELA-LITERACY.RST.11-12.5
- Integrating information from diverse media sources
  CCSS.ELA-LITERACY.RST.11-12.7

Student Perspective: "*It's great to replace some parts of our textbook and worksheets with articles, field manuals, and even some blog posts. I learned the information, but I also became familiar with people and publications that are important in this field.*"

Part of a library in an early childhood education classroom

Know Your Target Market

"I wish my students would create media and writing they could use in the real world, not just projects meant to earn them a grade!"

Gist: Students analyze a professional website, advertisement, or product packaging to determine the target market, listing the ways in which the product is meant to appeal to a specific group. Then, when students begin their own writing/creating, they use their lists to ensure that their product fits their own target audience.

When to use: Before beginning any writing, presenting, or creative media project. To identify possible professional uses, audiences, and appropriate style. When you want them to practice using expert vocabulary in context.

The Why

As quick as: 30 minutes

Multiple learning styles:

How It Works

Step 1: Have students work in small groups or pairs. Assign each group a product, advertisement, or professional website. Or challenge each student to find their own at home or online. Anything that has some professional writing on it should work!

Step 2: Groups or pairs should spend about 10 minutes discussing their product(s) using the following list of questions and taking notes.
1. Where was your product/advertisement/writing placed? Why?
2. Who is likely to read/view this product?
3. Is this product meant for people in a certain age group or level of expertise? How do you know?
4. Is this product/writing aimed at people of a certain social class or culture? How do you know?
5. How formal or informal is the writing? What does that tell you?
6. Are there any visual cues (color, fonts, images) that tell you something about the intended audience?
7. Is there any technical language used in this writing/media?
8. Choose a new audience for this product. How might you change the design and writing to appeal to this new audience?

Walk around and listen to your students as they discuss these questions, guiding and prompting where needed. Remember, it isn't important for them to tell YOU all their answers. It is important for them to talk through them with each other.

Step 3: Before students begin their own writing, create a presentation, or design a website, have them refer to these notes, and instruct them to answer the following questions before they begin:
1. Where could this writing/media be placed or seen, besides school?
2. Who is likely to read/view this product?
3. Do I want my writing/media to appeal to people in a specific age group or with a certain level of expertise?
4. Do I want my writing/media to appeal to a certain social class or culture group?
5. How formal or informal does my project need to be?
6. What visual cues (fonts, colors, images) could I use to appeal to my desired audience?
7. What technical language (if any) should I include in my writing?

Step 4: After answering these seven questions, they are ready to begin. You can break this activity into two halves, repeating only the first half (analyzing the intended audience) any time you read a text. Other times you may repeat only the second half, using these seven questions repeatedly, every time your students prepare to create, write, or present anything.

Student Perspective: "I never realized that my work could have a purpose outside of school. Now I'm creating writing I can use to market myself in the future!"

Common Core Connection

- Write discipline-focused arguments
  CCSS.ELA-LITERACY.WHST.11-12.1
- Write formally while attending to the norms and conventions of the discipline
  CCSS.ELA-LITERACY.WHST.11-12.1.D
- Write informative/explanatory texts
  CCSS.ELA-LITERACY.WHST.11-12.2
- Use precise language and domain-specific vocabulary
  CCSS.ELA-LITERACY.WHST.11-12.2D

Informational Speech

"I want my students to apply their professional knowledge in the way they talk about relevant issues."

The Gist: Students apply academic learning to a practical issue and deliver a professional speech or public service announcement that could be used professionally.

When to use: For a summative project after extensive classroom learning, to make the learning practical.

The Why

As quick as: extended

Multiple learning styles:

How It Works

Step 1: Introduce a practical issue that is relevant to your discipline.

Step 2: Remind students of the information they have studied through text, video, demonstrations, discussions, etc. Say, "Now, I want you to figure out how the facts you have learned apply to this issue. In a group, synthesize the important points you have learned about [topic] into one informational speech on the issue." Consider providing blank graphic organizers, notecards, and a timeline for students to use for planning.

Step 3: Remind students of the thought process detailed in "Know Your Target Market," page 182. Say, "Your presentation may be delivered as an overview to explain the topic, or as a public service announcement. Either way, it should include a professional tone."

Step 4: Later, when students deliver their speeches, have them use the speech summary chart on page 187 as they listen. They should determine key topics of each speech, and then collaborate to determine the overall themes of classmates' speeches.

Student Perspective: "I chose a CTE school because I want my learning to be practical, not just busy work. Learning to give a speech like an expert fits my purpose."

Example: In a culinary classroom, have students deliver a PSA about the potential hazards of eating food from buffet lines. Remind them of the various lessons they've completed that included facts about foodborne pathogens, sanitation, the spread of TCL foods, and restaurant industry practices. Point them to sections of their notes that may come in handy. Explain that in your industry, they will need to be able to discuss this topic comfortably in detail. In addition to the seven guiding questions listed in Know Your Target Market (p. 182), have students consider the following:

- What information can I include beyond what is in the text?
- What do I observe while watching people prepare and maintain a buffet?
- What do I observe while watching people eat from a buffet?
- How can I use the flow of food and my knowledge of providing safe food?
- How can I use a graphic organizer (cause/effect, flow chart) to explain the issue?
- Can I create a visual aid to make the danger of germs easier for the public to see?
- Which technical language is familiar to the public?

Common Core Connection

- Cite textual evidence
  CCSS.ELA-LITERACY.RST.11-12.1
- Summarize complex concepts by paraphrasing
  CCSS.ELA-LITERACY.RST.11-12.2
- Synthesize information from various sources into a coherent understanding
  CCSS.ELA-LITERACY.RST.11-12.9
- Write informative/explanatory texts
  CCSS.ELA-LITERACY.WHST.11-12.2
- Use precise language and domain-specific vocabulary
  CCSS.ELA-LITERACY.WHST.11-12.2D

Informational Speech Sample Rubric

Note: If you choose to use this activity as a graded assignment, consider using the questions below as your rubric, to ensure that you are assessing a student's thought process and professional habits of mind in addition to the outcome. Be sure to add or remove requirements per the standards of your own discipline.

Student must be able to answer "yes" to the following questions.

- Do you have a presentation that includes the Essential Question, at least 3 subtopics, the roles of each member in the group, and a timeline for completing the presentation?
- Have you used graphic organizers to synthesize the information learned in multiple classes?
- Do you have an outline or note cards to use during your speech?
- Do you explain where you learned the information used in your speech?
- Do you have visual aids to illustrate what you say in your speech?
- Is your group's presentation at least 10 minutes long and is your part of the speech at least 3-5 minutes long?

Get "Presentation Literate"!

Check out resources from former CTE teacher Rachael Mann, who founded Speak Like TED. Mann teaches "presentation literacy," helping students to develop a professional voice. Her speaking schedule and many other resources are on her site (scan below).

Left: Rachael Mann's main website

Right: Rachael Mann's CTE discussions on ACTEonline.org

Speech Summary Chart

Individual Summary Chart	
Speech #1: Key Topic/Idea	**Speech #2: Key Topic/Idea**
Speech #3: Key Topic/Idea	**Speech #4: Key Topic/Idea**
Collaborative Summary:	
Speech #4: Key Topic/Idea	**Speech #5: Key Topic/Idea**
Speech #6: Key Topic/Idea	**Speech #7: Key Topic/Idea**
Collaborative Summary:	

Punch the Holes in It

"I want my students to troubleshoot and think, not just complete another fill-in-the-blank quiz."

The Gist: Students watch an amateur how-to video on YouTube. They deconstruct the video, "punching holes" in its weak spots by noting any flaws, incomplete steps, incorrect procedures, or unclear communication.

When to Use: As a check for understanding or to assess prior knowledge, as an alternative to a worksheet or quiz. To assess understanding and applying information in context, rather than conditioning students to simply memorize facts. To reinforce professional norms.

The Why

As quick as: 15 minutes

Multiple learning styles:

Besides improving their content knowledge, students learn to read websites closely and evaluate credibility of online sources.

How It Works

Step 1 (before class): Search YouTube for amateur how-to videos on your topic of choice. (You could keep a file on your computer in which to store links to these types of videos whenever you come across one.) For example, in an electrician's class, you may show a video about how to wire a house. See the next page for a sample electrical wiring lesson and video link.

Step 2: Tell students, "Critique this video. Write your name on your paper, then take notes individually, listing any incomplete steps, incorrect or unsafe procedures, or ways the YouTuber miscommunicated or was unclear."

Step 3: Show the video to the whole class (try to keep it under 8 minutes or so, since our brains don't easily focus for longer than that).

Step 4: After the video, divide students into groups of 3 or 4. Say, "You have 5 minutes to create one list of ways you would improve the video, using all your individual lists. For each item that needs improvement, you should note a reason. (Example: The ladder should be wooden, not metal - metal conducts electricity [safety hazard])

Step 5: Walk around and listen to students as they create their master lists. You'll get a general understanding of how much information they have assimilated just by listening.

Step 6: For further assessment, groups should turn in their master lists, along with their individual note pages. With names on their papers, you can see how many and which types of flaws each student was able to catch in the video. There is no need to grade these assessments: their purpose is simply to tell you what your students have learned.

Twist: Expand this activity by having the student groups create their own how-to video or live demonstration using their master lists to improve upon the video they watched as a class.

Twist 2: Expand this activity by challenging students to find other videos that contain mistakes and share them with the class. Be sure to save these in your personal file for future use!

Common Core Connection

- Cite textual evidence
  CCSS.ELA-LITERACY.RST.11-12.1
- Summarize complex concepts by paraphrasing
  CCSS.ELA-LITERACY.RST.11-12.2
- Analyze author's purpose and identify unresolved issues
  CCSS.ELA-LITERACY.RST.11-12.6
- Evaluate hypotheses, data, analysis, and conclusions; verify data and corroborate or challenge conclusions with other evidence
  CCSS.ELA-LITERACY.RST.11-12.8
- Use precise language and domain-specific vocabulary
  CCSS.ELA-LITERACY.WHST.11-12.2D

Student Perspective: "I feel respected because my teacher knows I'm capable of using my knowledge in the real world instead of just on worksheets."

Making Claims and Accusations
Electrical Wiring Lesson
By Jon Capps, teacher in Fort Wayne, Indiana

Use this lesson with a video that contains mistakes, such as the video linked to the left, called "My wife is now an electrician! Annissa is wiring the house."

Option 1: Watch the youtube video linked here, with students noting inconsistencies, mistakes, safety hazards, and any other problems with the video. This video contains at least a dozen mistakes. You can even have students analyze the written details and comments below the video, looking for mistakes in the product list.

Option 2: Have students find their own videos. Give them the following assignment:

We all know there are a lot of DIY (Do It Yourself) people in our industry that claim to do everything under the sun. Some know what they are doing and others just clearly do not. Your task is to search the Internet and find a 3-5 min video produced by a DIY person.
Once you have found a "how-to" video you want to watch, take notes over the video. You may want to watch it 3 or more times, because you are likely to catch more mistakes with each viewing.
You will want notes on the good practices you see in the video as well as incorrect or misinformation given. Take good notes and pay close attention.
You will each present your video tomorrow to the class, discussing the claims, accusations, and mistakes you found.

Reading Schematics, Diagrams, and Blueprints (Text Features)

Gist: Students chart information from one of their textbook's diagrams or images to practice using text features for learning.

When to use: Early in the school year, to introduce students to the particular differences between text in their chosen discipline and other text they may be used to.

For many students, a CTE textbook provides a first introduction to the importance of diagrams, images, and charts. They may be in the habit of ignoring such features in other academic reading that is more verbal-reliant. If your textbook relies on image features, be explicit in teaching students to use them.

The Why

As quick as: 20 minutes

Multiple learning styles:

Metacognition (thinking about thinking): Understanding charts, diagrams, and other text features helps students get to know how they learn best.

How It Works

Step 1. Select a section of text that includes text features such as diagrams or images. For example, any given page in a construction text might be ¾ filled with illustrations of proper tool handling. In automotive texts, there will be exploded views of vehicles. Choose a section that includes these features relating to your current topic.

Step 2. Divide students into groups of 3 or 4. Distribute a copy of the comparison matrix (p.193) to each group. (Alternatively, have each group create their own large version on chart paper or on the board with Post-it notes to engage bodily-kinesthetic learners.)

Step 3. Say, "As a group, your task is to create a chart that might be used to compare the features or attributes of [items in the text]. You should use images or diagrams from the text to gather information and come up with items to compare (across the top) and attributes they may share (down the side). But DO NOT fill in your chart." Show an example of this type of chart so they know what you mean. (See example on the facing page.) If you have struggling students, you can model how to create this chart.

For example: In a construction class, students might compare different types of tools. They would list types of tools across the top of the chart. Then they would list possible attributes down the left-hand side, such as jobs they could be used for, or phrases like "Requires a GFCI," "Must have at every job," "Power-tool," and "Multi-purpose."

Step 4. Now have student groups switch charts so that each group is working with a chart created by another group. Say, "Now your task is to work together to fill in the chart you've been given. In the boxes that align an item with its attributes, place a check mark in the tiny checkbox. Then go back to all checked boxes and record notes on similarities and differences between items that share the same attribute. Use your textbooks to find the answers, and discuss with your group members. Look for information in the diagrams and images of the textbook, not only in the words."

Step 5. Facilitate discussion within groups as you walk among them. Ideally there will be some ambiguity as to whether certain attributes apply to some items. This makes for good discussion and deeper thinking.

Student Perspective: "I never stopped to take time to examine diagrams while reading until my teacher pointed out that in this career field visual diagrams are essential to thinking and communicating."

A student-made comparison matrix shows types of masonry jointers.

But I'm Not a Reading Teacher!

Common Core Connection

- Cite textual evidence
  CCSS.ELA-LITERACY.RST.11-12.1
- Analyze how text structures information into categories or hierarchies
  CCSS.ELA-LITERACY.RST.11-12.5
- Evaluate hypotheses, data, analysis, and conclusions; verify data and corroborate or challenge conclusions with other evidence
  CCSS.ELA-LITERACY.RST.11-12.8
- Work toward proficient independent understanding of text
  CCSS.ELA-LITERACY.RST.11-12.10
- Use precise language and domain-specific vocabulary
  CCSS.ELA-LITERACY.WHST.11-12.2D

Familiarity with text features is crucial to disciplinary literacy.

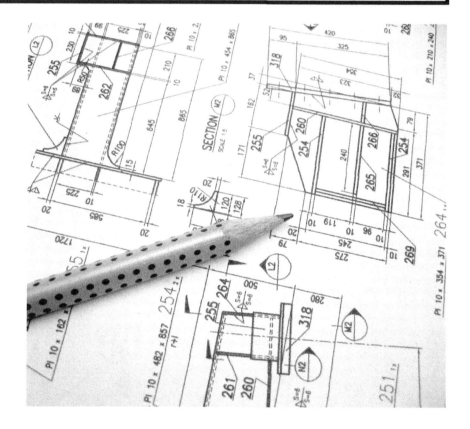

Comparison Matrix

Characteristics	Items to be compared		
	#1	#2	#3
1.	Similarities ☐ Differences	Similarities ☐ Differences	Similarities ☐ Differences
2.	Similarities ☐ Differences	Similarities ☐ Differences	Similarities ☐ Differences
3.	Similarities ☐ Differences	Similarities ☐ Differences	Similarities ☐ Differences
4.	Similarities ☐ Differences	Similarities ☐ Differences	Similarities ☐ Differences

Examining Ethics

"Students get bored during lessons about industry regulations, and they have not thought deeply about our discipline's particular ethics questions."

Gist: Students read an article or watch a video segment, then discuss the ethical implications with an eye toward their own future in the field.

When to use: When teaching industry regulations, couple the dry text of rules and standards with an ethics lesson to make the text more practical and memorable.

How It Works

Step 1 (before class): Find a relevant news article, or even a criminal law case, that has to do with the legal text you are teaching. For example, an IT class may read this linked article about digital animation technology that uses real actors' images, making it possible to create movies using deceased actors. (Scan code at left; See corresponding discussion questions on the next page.)

Step 2: Distribute the text of the related safety regulations or standards alongside the news article.

The Why

As quick as: 30 minutes

Multiple learning styles:

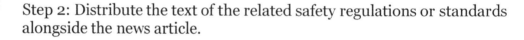

Step 3: Challenge groups of students to annotate the news article, labeling specific sections of it with the legal text that applies in some way.

Step 4: Distribute discussion questions about ethics, or use question stems (p.108) for students to create their own questions.

Step 5: Facilitate discussion. Use the news article as an entry into deeper questions of where technology might lead to future ethics dilemmas. Be sure to explore "gray areas" of the law, and ask students to point out any ethical dilemmas that are not regulated but come up in the news article.

Twist: Have students create a T-chart or other graphic organizer that shows specifically how the practical example corresponds to the regulation text.

> **Common Core Connection**
>
> - Cite textual evidence
>   CCSS.ELA-LITERACY.RST.11-12.1
> - Summarize complex concepts by paraphrasing
>   CCSS.ELA-LITERACY.RST.11-12.2
> - Determine meaning of key terms as used in context
>   CCSS.ELA-LITERACY.RST.11-12.4
> - Analyze how text structures information into categories or hierarchies
>   CCSS.ELA-LITERACY.RST.11-12.5
> - Analyze author's purpose and identify unresolved issues
>   CCSS.ELA-LITERACY.RST.11-12.6
> - Synthesize information from various sources into a coherent understanding
>   CCSS.ELA-LITERACY.RST.11-12.9
> - Work toward proficient independent understanding of text
>   CCSS.ELA-LITERACY.RST.11-12.10
> - Use precise language and domain-specific vocabulary
>   CCSS.ELA-LITERACY.WHST.11-12.2D

Examining Ethics - Sample Critical Thinking Questions

These questions correspond to the CBS News article "Digital Doubles."

1. This article began with the concept of being innovative. Using evidence from the text, what would you identify as the top 5 traits it takes to be innovative?

2. Who's more innovative: the team that created the advanced Light Stage at Creative Technologies or Ari Shapiro, who used the $100 cameras and shower curtain to create the makeshift capture lab? How can you defend your choice?

3. Toward the end, the author brings up virtual clones. The author poses the question, "But how long will it take until someone tries to use a virtual clone of a person for an unethical or questionable reason?"
    a. In what situations could you imagine people manipulating this technology for unethical purposes. Can you think of 3-4 possible "wrong" reasons someone might use virtual clones?
    b. Outside of Hollywood, can you think of 3-4 other positive potential uses of virtual clones?

4. At the end, the author says that politicians, creative types, policy makers, and practitioners should all be brought to the table to work together in creating virtual cloning laws. If you had to prove that this kind of technology needs to be regulated, what are 3-4 other innovative techniques from the recent past that you could use to make your point?

Professional Work Ethic

"I want my students to take initiative, work hard, and develop agency in thinking and communicating professionally."

Gist: Students brainstorm attributes of professionalism in general and in the discipline specifically. Then they develop their own rubric for assessing professional work ethic in future class projects.

When to use: When your students need help thinking of themselves as future professionals and seeing how their actions now will affect their careers.

How It Works

The Why

As quick as: 40 minutes

Multiple learning styles:

Step 1. Start with the "12 Who Mattered" activity (p.198). Allow 1 minute for students to fill in the first 6 boxes with people who display an exemplary work ethic. Then, untimed, have students fill in the remaining 6 boxes with peers in the room who have shown a good work ethic in some way, big or small.

Step 2. Allow students to walk around and see whom others came up with, then begin a discussion of their choices, asking for examples of how the person displayed a good work ethic.

Step 3. Introduce the idea of professionalism, writing the word on the board. Ask students to look back at their 12 boxes and find people who showed professionalism in general (in any field).

Step 4. Using the names listed, brainstorm general attributes of professionalism in any field. Then move into brainstorming what professionalism means to those in your field specifically. You may want to have students make a T-chart on the board, listing general professional attributes on the left, and listing professional attributes that are specific to your discipline on the right.

Step 5. Distribute the work ethic rubric (p.199), and read it with the class. Use the Scaffolded Questions for Discussion (p.200) to guide your students through the rubric.

Step 6. Have students adapt the general work ethic rubric to your class specifically, adding specific measures of professionalism within the discipline. They will work together to create their own rubric for your class, using the ideas they brainstormed on the T-chart, both general and specific.

Step 7. Have students create a visual display of their new Professional Work Ethic Rubric for the classroom. Encourage them to make it look professional, using images if appropriate to your discipline.

Step 8. Use the student-created rubric for assessment, self-assessment, and peer-review during collaborative projects throughout the year.

Twist: Have students write a short statement (3 sentences or less) on an exit card explaining what it means to have a professional work ethic in your discipline. (For more on exit cards, see page 82). If your students create a website or portfolio, have them include this statement in it.

Student Perspective: "Using the rubric that we made ourselves makes me feel respected, like my teacher knows I can handle this. It makes me want to live up to the standards we wrote down."

Self-Directed Professionalism

Embracing disciplinary literacy pushes students toward learning that is increasingly self-directed. Emphasize the importance of taking initiative as they stake out a place for themselves in your field. Explain that professionalism is the "why" for learning to speak, write, read, listen, and think is ways that are specific to the discipline. By giving students a chance to define professionalism themselves and create their own assessment rubric, you are helping them take ownership of their professional future.

Common Core Connection

- Integrate and evaluate multiple diverse sources to solve a problem
  CCSS.ELA-LITERACY.RST.11-12.7
- Synthesize information from various sources into a coherent understanding
  CCSS.ELA-LITERACY.RST.11-12.9
- Establish a formal style; attend to norms and conventions of the discipline
  CCSS.ELA-LITERACY.WHST.11-12.1.D
- Use precise language and domain-specific vocabulary
  CCSS.ELA-LITERACY.WHST.11-12.2D

Twelve Who Mattered

Directions: There are 12 boxes below. You have exactly 1 minute to fill in the first 6 boxes with the name of a person whose life demonstrates this statement:

EFFORT = ACHIEVEMENT

The names can be anyone you know personally or have read about, living or dead.

You only need to be able to justify to the rest of us that they meet our "effort = achievement" criteria.

Only fill in the top 6 boxes…GO!

Part 3: Disciplinary Literacy

WORK ETHIC RUBRIC

Use this rubric (or your own if you have one) as a starting point for students to create their own professional work ethic rubric for your class.

PROFESSIONAL WORK ETHIC CRITERIA	EXCELLENT	ACCEPTABLE	UNACCEPTABLE
DEADLINES	Hands in work on time in high quality form.	Hands in work on time but had to rush to finish & the work quality has suffered.	Work not handed in on time.
PRODUCTIVITY	Listens and reads directions; able to work without supervision; works the entire time	Works on assigned projects, but must ask for extra instructions or concentration level varies	Must be told to get back to work or to begin working; distracts others.
PREPAREDNESS	Has proper materials every day; ready to participate in each day's activities.	Has proper materials but must scramble at times to get them; ready to participate	Borrowing or searching for material; not ready to participate.
TEAMWORK	Works toward achievement of group goals; promotes group interaction.	Works toward group goals and expresses ideas with prompting.	Does not work toward group goals; does not participate in group interaction.
COMMUNICATION	Listens and participates; follows written and oral directions; speaks and writes effectively 100% of the time.	Listens and participates; follows written and oral directions; speaks and writes effectively with some prompting.	Does not listen and/or participate; does not follow directions, does not express spoken or written language clearly.
RESPECTFULNESS	Frequently uses good manners and shows concern for others.	Generally uses good manners and show concern for others.	Seldom uses good manners or shows concern for others.

But I'm Not a Reading Teacher!

Scaffolded Questions for Work Ethic Rubric

Teacher's Guide: Scaffolding your questions allows students to build on their understanding and synthesis of the topics as you ask questions at different cognitive levels.

1. Who are the two people you heard mentioned in our "Twelve That Mattered" that you think really exemplify the best work ethic? (knowledge)
2. What did you use as your criteria to judge the people you included? (understanding)
3. In your own life, what are some behaviors you use to demonstrate your work ethic? (application)
4. Which 2-3 characteristics do you think best illustrate that someone has a good work ethic? (analysis)
5. Let's take 5 specific people and list them on the whiteboard. From your knowledge of these people and their achievements, what 2-3 key traits do you think they have in common? (synthesis)
6. Read the rubric. Which columns are you surprised to see as an evaluation of "work ethic"? How effective do you think these criteria are for measuring work ethic? (evaluation)
7. If you had to add a column to the work ethic criteria, what is a trait that could improve this rubric? (creation)
8. What are specific criteria we could add to tailor this rubric to our professional discipline? (creation)

Have students circle the sections to assess themselves in each category. Use updated rubric as a discussion tool, a growth tool to revisit throughout the year, or as a peer assessment tool for projects.

APPENDIX A

CHOOSING COMPLEX TEXT

A 2006 report released by ACT, Inc., revealed data showing that students were disproportionately missing questions that are based on complex texts. So when students did not achieve a "benchmark" on the ACT Reading Test, the cause was less likely to be a lack of academic skills in general and more likely to be an inability to read and understand complex text in particular. Over the next several years, "text complexity" would become a big deal for teachers.

But what exactly does "complexity" mean? It's not quite the same as "difficulty." Identifying complexity requires more than simply asking, "Can my students read at this level?" The ACT determines the complexity of a text by looking at six aspects of the text and determining whether each aspect is straightforward or intricate:

1. **Relationships** (interactions among ideas or characters)
2. **Richness** (amount and sophistication of information conveyed through data or literary devices)
3. **Structure** (how the text is organized and how it progresses)
4. **Style** (author's tone and use of language)
5. **Vocabulary** (author's word choice)
6. **Purpose** (author's intent in writing the text)

(ACT, 2006)

If you choose texts for your students based only on "difficulty," or by simply getting a feel for complexity when you read through it, consider adopting a more procedural approach. When you're looking for complex texts to use in your classroom, think through the above six aspects. Look for texts that contain the following:

1. Subtle or deeply embedded relationships between ideas
2. Richness in data or details
3. Elaborate or unconventional organization
4. Intricate style or unexpected tone
5. A context-dependent vocabulary
6. An implied or ambiguous purpose

APPENDIX B

MULTIPLE INTELLIGENCES TEST

Adapted from Howard Gardner's original Multiple Intelligences assessment.

Howard Gardner's research on Multiple Intelligences names 7 Dominant Intelligences:

1. Verbal-Linguistic Intelligence
2. Logical-Mathematical Intelligence
3. Musical-Rhythmic Intelligence
4. Spatial Intelligence
5. Bodily-Kinesthetic Intelligence
6. Interpersonal Intelligence
7. Intrapersonal Intelligence

Quickly read the following statements and check each statement that applies to you.

_____1. I easily remember nice turns of phrase or memorable quotes and use hem deftly in conversation.

_____2. My library of books is among my most precious possessions.

_____3. I can hear words in my head before I read, speak or write them down.

_____4. I get more out of listening to news on the radio and hearing books on cassette than I do from watching TV.

_____5. I am a master when t comes to word games like Scrabble, Anagrams, and Password.

_____6. I enjoy entertaining others with tongue twisters, nonsense, rhymes or puns.

_____7. Other people sometimes have to stop and ask me to explain the meaning of words I use in my writing and speaking.

_____8. English, social studies and history were easier for me in school than math and science.

_____9. When I drive down a freeway, I pay more attention to the words written in the billboards than to the scenery.

_____10. My conversation is peppered with frequent references to things that I have read.

_____11. I have written something recently that I was particularly proud of or that earned me special recognition by others.

_____12. I note people's errors in using words or grammar, even if I don't correct them.

_____13. I am fascinated by scientific and philosophical questions like "When did time begin?"

_____14. I can easily double or triple a cooking recipe or carpentry measurement without having to put it all down on paper.

_____15. Math and science were among my favorite subjects in school.

_____16. I frequently beat my friends in chess, checks, Go or other strategy games.

_____17. I like to set up little "what if" experiments (eg, What if I double the amount of plant food that I feed to my plants at home?)

_____18. People sometimes tell me that I have a very computer-like mind.

_____19. I organize things in my kitchen, bathroom, and at my desk according to categories and in patterns.
_____20. I believe that almost everything has a certain rational explanation.
_____21. I wonder a lot about how things work.
_____22. I like finding logical flaws in the things that people say and do at home and work.
_____23. I sometimes think in clear, abstract, wordless, imageless concepts.
_____24. I feel more comfortable when something has been measured, categorized, analyzed, or quantified.

_____25. I enjoy music and have favorite performers.
_____26. People say that I have a pleasant singing voice.
_____27. I can tell when a musical note is off key.
_____28. My collection of records, cassettes or CDs is among my most treasured possessions.
_____29. I play a musical instrument.
_____30. My life would be impoverished if there were no music in it.
_____31. I catch myself sometime walking down the street with a television jingle or other tune running obsessively through my mind.
_____32. I can easily keep time to a piece of music with a simple percussion instrument.
_____33. I know the tunes to many different songs or musical pieces.
_____34. If I hear a musical selection once or twice, I am usually able to sing it back fairly accurately.
_____35. I often make tapping sounds or sing melodies while working, studying or learning something new.
_____36. I sometimes enjoy different sounds in my environment.

_____37. I can remember in detail the layout and landmarks of places I've visited on vacation.
_____38. I often see clear visual images when I close my eyes.
_____39. I am usually sensitive to color.
_____40. I have a camera or camcorder that I use to record what I see around me.
_____41. I can easily solve jigsaw puzzles, mazes and other visual puzzles.
_____42. I sometimes have vivid dreams at night.
_____43. I can easily find my way around unfamiliar territory.
_____44. People praise me for the drawings or doodles I create.
_____45. Geometry was easier for me than algebra in school.
_____46. When I do artwork I seem to know just how to arrange the parts of the picture or product.
_____47. I can comfortably imagine how something might appear as it were looked down upon from directly above in a bird's eye view.
_____48. I prefer looking at a material that is heavily illustrated.

_____49. I regularly engage in at least one sport or physical activity.
_____50. I can master new sports easily.
_____51. I find it difficult to sit still for a long period of time.
_____52. I like working with my hand at some concrete activities such as swimming, weaving, carving, carpentry or model building.

_____53. My best ideas often come to me when I'm out for a walk or jog.
_____54. I like to spend my free time outdoors.
_____55. I frequently use hand gestures or other forms of body language when conversing with someone.
_____56. I need to touch things in order to learn more about them.
_____57. I enjoy scary movies; dare devil amusement rides or similarly thrilling experiences.
_____58. I would describe myself as well coordinated.
_____59. I need to practice a new skill by doing it rather than reading about it or seeing a video that describes it.
_____60. I often can figure out how something works or how to fix something that's broken, without asking for help.

_____61. When I meet new people, I often make connections between their characters and those of other acquaintances.
_____62. I'm considered the local dear Abby in my neighborhood and people often come to see me for help and advice.
_____63. I can sense quickly how other people are feeling about things and themselves.
_____64. I prefer group sports like badminton, volleyball or softball to solo sports like swimming and jogging.
_____65. When I have a problem, I'm more likely to seek out another person for help rather than attempt to work it out on my own.
_____66. I have at lest 3 close friends.
_____67. I prefer social pastimes like Monopoly, board games, and card games to playing video games or solitaire.
_____68. I enjoy the challenge of teaching another person what I know how to do.
_____69. People have called me a "born leader" before.
_____70. I feel comfortable in the middle of a crowd.
_____71. I like to get involved in social activities connected with my work, church or community.
_____72. I would rather spend my nights at a lively party than at home alone.

_____73. I regularly spend time alone to meditate, reflect, or think about important life questions.
_____74. I think about what I want from life and what I want to accomplish.
_____75. I have attended counseling sessions to learn more about myself.
_____76. I have intuitions (or gut feelings) about things that often turn out to happen.
_____77. People tend to see me as a loner.
_____78. I have a special hobby or interest that I keep pretty much to myself.
_____79. I have some important goals set for myself that I think about on a regular basis.
_____80. I prefer to spend a weekend alone in a cabin in the woods rather than go to a fancy resort with lots of people.
_____81. I usually know how I feel about something or about my feelings.
_____82. I keep a personal diary or journal to record the events of my inner life.
_____83. I am self-employed or at least have though about starting my own business.
_____84. I would rather spend my evenings at home than at a lively party.

ANSWER KEY

Below are the corresponding question sections for each intelligence with a brief description each. It is important to remember 2 key points when discussing MIs.

1. MI research changes the question from "How smart are you?" to "How are you smart?" In other words, we now recognize that all people have an intellectual strength, and that traditional education experiences heavily emphasize Verbal and Linguistic Intelligence development over the other five.
2. To have a strong MI actually highlights your Learning Style preferences and can be very helpful when a student is struggling with the delivery of content. Knowing your MI can help you rethink how you are currently trying to learn new skills and content.

- Verbal-Linguistic Intelligence
    - #1-12
    - Learning best with reading, writing and speaking
    - Usually a lover of words, quotes, speeches, etc
- Logical-Mathematical Intelligence
    - #13-24
    - Learning with procedures, processes, graphs, timelines, and logical sequencing
- Auditory-Rhythmic Intelligence
    - #25-36
    - Learning most naturally occurs with listening, watching videos, listening to music and rhythmic environments.
- Spatial Intelligence
    - #37-48
    - Learning within spatial intelligence involves use of manipulatives and models. These learners benefit from interacting directly with what they are learning.
- Bodily-Kinesthetic Intelligence
    - #49-60
    - Learning through bodily movements and active environments are best for these learners. Thinking occurs naturally with movement.
- Interpersonal Intelligence
    - #61-72
    - Collaboration, group work, partner work with structured dialogue and conversations allow this type of learner to digest the content and skills more easily.
- Intrapersonal Intelligence
    - #73-84

Intrapersonal learners learn naturally with time to reflect, consider, and think deeply about the content. Most people with this learning style blog or journal regularly.

APPENDIX C
Common Core English Language Arts Standards for Science and Technical Subjects

(Taken from corestandards.org)

Key Ideas and Details:

CCSS.ELA-LITERACY.RST.11-12.1 *Cite specific textual evidence to support analysis of science and technical texts, attending to important distinctions the author makes and to any gaps or inconsistencies in the account.*

CCSS.ELA-LITERACY.RST.11-12.2 *Determine the central ideas or conclusions of a text; summarize complex concepts, processes, or information presented in a text by paraphrasing them in simpler but still accurate terms.*

CCSS.ELA-LITERACY.RST.11-12.3 *Follow precisely a complex multistep procedure when carrying out experiments, taking measurements, or performing technical tasks; analyze the specific results based on explanations in the text.*

Craft and Structure:

CCSS.ELA-LITERACY.RST.11-12.4 *Determine the meaning of symbols, key terms, and other domain-specific words and phrases as they are used in a specific scientific or technical context relevant to grades 11-12 texts and topics.*

CCSS.ELA-LITERACY.RST.11-12.5 *Analyze how the text structures information or ideas into categories or hierarchies, demonstrating understanding of the information or ideas.*

CCSS.ELA-LITERACY.RST.11-12.6 *Analyze the author's purpose in providing an explanation, describing a procedure, or discussing an experiment in a text, identifying important issues that remain unresolved.*

Integration of Knowledge and Ideas:

CCSS.ELA-LITERACY.RST.11-12.7 *Integrate and evaluate multiple sources of information presented in diverse formats and media (e.g., quantitative data, video, multimedia) in order to address a question or solve a problem.*

CCSS.ELA-LITERACY.RST.11-12.8 *Evaluate the hypotheses, data, analysis, and conclusions in a science or technical text, verifying the data when possible and corroborating or challenging conclusions with other sources of information.*

CCSS.ELA-LITERACY.RST.11-12.9 *Synthesize information from a range of sources (e.g., texts, experiments, simulations) into a coherent understanding of a process, phenomenon, or concept, resolving conflicting information when possible.*

Range of Reading and Level of Text Complexity:

CCSS.ELA-LITERACY.RST.11-12.10 *By the end of grade 12, read and comprehend science/technical texts in the grades 11-CCR text complexity band independently and proficiently.*

REFERENCES

ACTE (2017). "About CTE." *Association for Career & Technical Education*. Retrieved from https://www.acteonline.org/aboutcte/#.WNK0KaK1vIU

BBC Worldwide (1998). "How we learn." *The human body* (documentary film). Retrieved from http://learningandtheadolescentmind.org/resources_02_learning.html

Beach, T. (2013). "What is 'overlearning' and why is it so important? *A+ Test Prep and Tutoring*. Published online October 21, 2013. Retrieved from http://www.aplustutoring.com/blog/news/what-is-overlearning-and-why-is-it-so-important

Beers, K. & Probst, R. (2012). *Notice & note: Strategies for close reading*. Portsmouth, NH: Heinemann.

Bickley, H. (2014). "What exactly is disciplinary literacy, anyway?" *Catapult Learning*. Jan 9, 2014. Retrieved From https://www.catapultlearning.com/exactly-disciplinary-literacy-anyway/

Bray, B. & McClaskey, K. (2016). "Continuum of voice: What it means for the learner." *PersonalizeLearning*, May 10, 2016. Retrieved from http://www.personalizelearning.com/2016/01/continuum-of-voice-what-it-means-for.html

Forget, M. A. (2004). *MAX teaching with reading and writing: Classroom activities to help students learn subject matter while acquiring new skills*. Trafford.

Hattie, J. (2009). *Visible learning: A synthesis of over 800 meta-analyses relating to achievement*. London: Routledge.

Hernandez, D. (2012). "How third-grade reading skills and poverty influence high school graduation." *The Annie E. Casey Foundation*. Retrieved from http://www.aecf.org/m/resourcedoc/AECF-DoubleJeopardy-2012-Full.pdf#page=3

I Six Sigma (2016). *Determine the root cause: 5 whys*. Retrieved in 2016 from https://www.isixsigma.com/tools-templates/cause-effect/determine-root-cause-5-whys/

Johnson, V. G. and Mongo, J. A. (2008). "Literacy across the curriculum in urban schools: teaching reading across the curriculum requires a culturally responsive pedagogy." *Leadership Compass* Vol. 5, No. 3, Spring 2008 Retrieved from https://www.naesp.org/resources/2/Leadership_Compass/2008/LC2008v5n3a2.pdf

Kohn, A. (2011). "The case against grades." *Educational Leadership*. November, 2011. Retrieved from http://www.alfiekohn.org/article/case-grades/

López-Barroso, D.; Catani, M.; Ripollés, P.; Dell'Acqua, F.; Rodriguéz-Fornells, A.; & Diego-Balaguer, R. (2013). "Word learning is mediated by the left arcuate fasciculus." *Proceedings of the National Academy of Sciences of the United States of America*. Published online July 24, 2013. Retrieved from https://www.ncbi.nlm.nih.gov/pmc/articles/PMC3740909/

McLaughlin, M. & DeVoogd, G. (2004). *Critical literacy: Enhancing students' comprehension of text*. New York: Scholastic.

Morrell, D. (1986). "Just how long is a trillion seconds?" *New York Times*, Sept. 18, 1986. Retrieved from http://www.nytimes.com/1986/09/28/opinion/l-just-how-long-is-a-trillion-seconds-229186.html

Myers, D. G., & DeWall, C. N. (2015). *Psychology*. New York: Worth

Overseas Schools Advisory Council, U.S. Department of State. (2004). Norms of collaborative work. Count me in: Developing inclusive international schools, 4th ed. chapter 5. Retrieved from http://www.state.gov/m/a/os/43984.htm

Rosenshine, B. (2012). "Principles of instruction: Research-based strategies that all teachers should know." *American Educator*. Spring, 2012.

Rutherford, M. (2014). *Artisan teacher*. RLG Press.

Shanahan T., Shanahan C. (2011). "What is disciplinary literacy and why does it matter?" *Topics in Language Disorders*. Retrieved from http://crlp.ucsc.edu/resources/downloads/Shanahan%20What%20is%20Disciplinary%20Literacy.pdf

Shermer, M. (2005). "The Feynman-Tufte principle." *Scientific American*. April 1, 2005. Retrieved from https://www.scientificamerican.com/article/the-feynman-tufte-princip/

Stanovich, K. E. (2009). *What Intelligence Tests Miss: The Psychology of Rational Thought*. New Haven: Yale University Press.

Stephens, G., Silbert, L. & Hasson, U. (2010). "Speaker-listener neural coupling underlies successful communication." *Proceedings of the National Academy of Sciences of the United States of America.* Retrieved from https://www.ncbi.nlm.nih.gov/pmc/articles/PMC2922522/

Sum, A.; Khatiwada, I.; McLaughlin, J.; and Palma, S. (2009). "The consequences of dropping out of high school: Joblessness and jailing for high school dropouts and the high cost for taxpayers." *Northeastern University*. Retrieved from https://www.prisonpolicy.org/scans/The_Consequences_of_Dropping_Out_of_High_School.pdf

WIDA Consortium: World-Class Instructional Design and Assessment (2012). *The English Language Learner Can Do Booklet.* Board of Regents of the University of Wisconsin System

INDEX

A

Agriculture 1, 11, 99,
Analyzing 6, 50, 91, 94, 124, 140, 178, 182
Annotation 24, 173
Arcuate fasciculus 90
Assessment vocabulary 87
Automotive 1, 54, 91, 134, 137, 158, 190

B

Big ideas (disciplinary literacy) 153
Blended learning 3, 140
Brainstorming 110, 114, 120, 124, 128, 134, 140
Bureau of Labor Statistics, 84
Busy work 10, 82, 92, 93, 184

C

Categorizing 50-51, 66, 68-70, 89, 95, 103, 110, 180
Cause and effect 128, 134, 142
Chart paper 46, 64, 66, 96, 120, 140, 190,
Chunking 3, 4, 9, 30, 173
Clipboards 19, 55, 70, 95, 104, 124
Close reading four-break process 173
Common Core State Standards 2, 6, 10, 91, 206
Complexity and simplicity 12, 81
Construction 32, 83, 166, 168, 190
Cosmetology 2, 11, 64, 66, 92, 109, 149, 165
CTE advantage, the 3
Culinary 12, 55, 100, 174, 179, 185,
Diagnosing problems 54, 74-79, 134, 151, 177

D

Differentiation 37, 70, 161
Digital literacy 84
Dry erase boards 69, 95

E

Early childhood education 2, 68-69, 124, 155, 181
Electrical 21, 84, 90, 135-136, 188-189
EMT 2, 142
Essential questions 44, 91, 99, 153
Equity 4, 97-98

F

Feynman, Richard 12
Fishbowl, 106
Feedback 4-5, 11, 92, 104-105, 144
Forget, Mark A. 32, 168

G

Gardner, Howard 202
Gillie, Karen 38
Grades, de-emphasizing 92
Graphic organizers 4
Graphic representations 19, 38, 81

H

Habits of mind (disciplinary literacy) 177
Habituation 3, 4, 7, 9, 16, 20, 100,
Hands-On learning 2, 3
Hattie, John 15, 91, 145
HVAC 5, 84

I

Incidental vocabulary 87
Information Technology (IT) 6, 165, 194

K

Kahoot 42

L

Learning styles 2, 8
Library, classroom 6, 180
Literacy
    content area 1
    disciplinary 1, 147
    outcomes 1, 91-92
    skills list 7
    understanding 6

M

Masonry 191
Medical science 64, 165, 172-173
Metacognition 10, 92-93
Mind mapping 94
Multiple intelligences 202

N

Neural pathways 91

O

Overlearning 91

P

Popsticks 95
Post-It notes 95
Prediction 4, 26, 28, 32, 144, 168, 170
Problem-solving (see diagnosing problems)
Productive talk 1, 89
Professional learning 144
Professionalism 174, 194, 196

Q

Question stems, 108-109
Questions, generating thoughtful p. 99, 106
Quizlet 42

R

Rosenshine Barak 43
Rubrics 92, 158-159, 186, 196, 199-200

S

Scaffolding 45, 68, 69, 70, 85, 196, 200
Serial position effect 41
Sofia Tree Productions 44
Standards (see Common Core State Standards)
SWRL 9, 16, 73, 90

T

Text
    complex 201
    rethinking the definition of 6
Tools, physical 4, 95

V

Van, "Simplify" 81

W

Welding 71
Whiteboards (see dry erase boards)

Made in the USA
Columbia, SC
14 June 2023

18069481R00124